Silopi: A True Story of Love and Resilience

Bradford J. Beyer

Defiance Press & Publishing, LLC

DEFIANCE PRESS
& PUBLISHING

Silopi: A True Story of Love and Resilience
By Bradford J. Beyer
© 2024 All rights reserved.

The information in this book is provided for general informational purposes only and does not constitute legal, medical, or other professional advice. While the author and publisher have made every effort to ensure the accuracy of the information contained herein, they assume no responsibility for errors or omissions or for any actions taken based on the contents of this book. Readers should consult a qualified professional for advice tailored to their individual needs.

Published by:
Defiance Press & Publishing, LLC
www.defiancepress.com

ISBN:
eBook: 978-1-963102-95-6
Paperback: 978-1-963102-96-3
Printed in the United States of America

For permission requests or inquiries, contact Defiance Press & Publishing at:
publishing@defiancepress.com

Dedication

I dedicate this book to my wonderful wife.
There are many more words I could use to
describe how great you are, but I know
you would never let me list them all.
Thank you for encouraging me to write this story
and thank you for being the best part of my life.

Foreword

T he story you are about to read was actually written more than thirty years ago, but it was not committed to paper until now. The process of putting pen to paper began in the winter of 2023 when my wife and I decided to finally start our purge. It was just after Christmas, a time when many people begin the arduous task of removing the decorations they put out weeks earlier. In our case, it was time to pack away the decorations that I annually accuse my wife of putting out in late July. In reality, we begin decorating in mid-November each year. Part of this stems from the fact that, for some reason, we put up four Christmas trees in our home each year, and the decorating takes a bit of time.

Growing up in my family, we always knew when the party was over. My wife still laughs about her first Christmas with my family. After the presents were all opened and the post-party hangover began to sink in, she was shocked when my sisters and mother dutifully jumped to their feet, began throwing away the discarded wrapping paper, and the vacuum whirred to life. It seems she was unused to the joys of post-party cleanup that were passed along through my genetic lineage. During her upbringing, this was a time when her family would lie around and bask in the glow of the Christmas tree lights like gators on an embankment along the Tamiami Trail in southwest Florida. Since her baptism by vacuum so many years ago, she now reports after every gathering we host, "I love being a Beyer." This mantra is always uttered as the last of the dishes are placed in the dishwasher, the final inch of carpet is swept, and the Shark Steam Mop is returned to its rightful place after a tour of our hardwood floors.

As the son of a mother with obsessive-compulsive tendencies, if you must have a mental illness, at least you have one that results in a clean and tidy home. This familial compulsiveness also resulted in a childhood where our Christmas tree seemed to come down at the same speed as the New Year's Ball in Times Square. In January of 2023, my wife and I vowed, as we put away our Christmas decorations, that this year would be the year of the 'Purge.' For us, this meant that after we began replacing our Christmas totes to their rightful place for another year, we would start going through our home and getting rid of everything we no longer used or needed.

As a team, we began exploring closets and storage rooms that had gathered the remnants of our lives together. Clothes were donated, and trash was deposited at the street as we touched everything we owned and assessed whether it remained valuable or was destined for disposal. The house literally seemed to exhale as trash bag after trash bag was carried down the driveway and truckload after truckload was driven to our local Salvation Army. What had started as our 'Purge' was soon referred to as our 'Death Cleaning.' This new description came midway through the process when my wife read an article about the Swedish organizational task known as 'Death Cleaning.' Apparently, this somber-sounding term refers to the late-middle-aged activity of cleaning and decluttering your home before you die as a means of sparing your surviving family members such a large undertaking.

And so, weekend after weekend, we pulled totes from our storage rooms, perused their contents, and slimmed down our personal belongings. I teased my wife as I continued to remove plastic bins labeled as her 'Treasures,' 'Memories,' and 'Work Papers.' Apparently, women—or at least my woman—harbor an underlying desire to save every photo album, every high school trinket, and of course, their sorority paddle, the function of which I cannot even begin to understand. Still, she diligently went through one tote after another, reluctantly disposing of the memories she was willing to cast aside at that moment. Then, as I removed yet another tote labeled 'Old Memories,' I readied myself for another smart aleck comment about the baggage she brought into our marriage. However, as I peeled off the lid of this particular tote, I immediately saw a squashed camouflage hat adorned with a Specialist E-4 pin. It was then that I realized I had stumbled into my own bin of memories from a previous life. Of course, I did not bring to her attention that I had tapped into a tote of my own junk. Why give her any ammunition to fire back at me?

In addition to old pictures of Philadelphia Phillies ballplayers, Star Wars and G.I. Joe comic books, and wooden Pinewood Derby racers, I found the remnants of my life in the United States Army. There were the medals I had been awarded, a photo album filled with pictures taken at Basic Training and during my overseas assignments, countless envelopes of letters I had sent home to my parents that they had saved, and a binder stuffed with all kinds of military documents. Among these forgotten mementos, I found a picture of her. I have told her story many times over the years; in fact, my wife told me years ago that this story was one of the things that made her fall in love with me. I held up the picture so that my wife could see. In a way that only she can, my wife tilted her head and let out a small "Aww." This was quickly followed by a refrain she has stated countless times over the years: "I'm telling you, you need to write her story." Interestingly, my wife added to her traditional argument this time as we stood in our basement. Looking at me, she commented on how the country could use a story like this one.

Growing up in the seventies and eighties, both my wife and I were children of television and movies. We grew up when TV was a staple in the household. Shows like Diff'rent Strokes, Happy Days, Laverne & Shirley, The Facts of Life, The Dukes of Hazzard, Three's Company, Sanford and Son, Mork & Mindy, Good Times, The Jeffersons, and countless Warner Brothers cartoons influenced our upbringing as much as the lessons our parents taught us about life. And of course, who could forget The Brady Bunch? When I first met my wife, we immediately bonded over our shared love for this show as we discussed Marcia getting hit in the nose with the football, Jan wishing she had no brothers or sisters, and the kids singing as the 'Silver Platters' as they tried to win a $100 gift for their parents. So touched was I by this show that my mother frequently recounts how I referred to my family by the Brady Bunch names from ages two to three. My older sister Mandy became 'Cindy,' my older brother Drew became 'Bobby,' and my poor oldest sister Robin, for some unexplained reason, became 'Alice,' the maid. Of course, I ordained myself as 'Greg,' the oldest and coolest of the Brady clan.

While my mother understandably came to be called "Mrs. Brady," my father simply took on the moniker of "Mike." Over the years, my mother has reminded me how I never slipped and reverted to normal family names for an entire year. Even more humorous was the fact that I was able to push my father, perhaps the most easygoing man to have ever walked this planet, into near rage by calling out to him in public as "Mike." My mom recounts the time when my father's filament finally popped in the middle of a store, and he informed me in no uncertain terms that he would no longer respond to me if I didn't start calling him "Dad."

Like any kids growing up in the seventies and eighties, my wife and I could tell you the television lineup for that evening based on the day of the week. In recent years, we have lamented how television has all but died. In fact, we are hard-pressed to identify a current television drama or sitcom, let alone what day of the week it is televised. But before you blame this on the notion that we are simply getting old, it is important to note that our two teenage sons never even watch television outside of sports games. Instead, they watch YouTube or TikTok videos. This realization led to an official divorce from our satellite service years earlier. Sadly, it appears that Hollywood has followed the same disheartening trajectory.

To demonstrate this observation, as I began to type these first words, my sons and their friends were on their way to watch a movie called Cocaine Bear, the true story of a bear that overdosed on a satchel of cocaine dropped from an airplane during a drug shipment. A quick review of the media guide prior to their departure revealed that the R rating was assigned to the film due to the incessant use of the F-word and the frequent gory and bloody mauling of human beings at the hands of a coked-out Yogi. Unfortunately, the only other two viable options for their viewing pleasure that night were Raiders of the Lost Ark (a film released 42 years earlier) and Titanic (which is now celebrating its 26th anniversary). In addition to serving up these theatrical leftovers as a means of filling up screen space, we have all been subjected to remake after remake. In fact, a quick Google search identified, in 2018, a list of 121 remakes in the works. The list included the revamping of movies like Dune, Scream, the Texas Chainsaw Massacre, Firestarter, Father of the Bride, Clueless, Fletch, and for some reason, Every Which Way but Loose. In short, it appears that Hollywood has given up on creativity in exchange for an unending refurbishment of old stories. What you are about to read in the following pages is my humble attempt to add to the small, but hopefully growing, list of original stories. I hope you enjoy it.

Contents

1. HOME   1

2. ENLISTMENT   19

3. FORT BENNING   29

4. GRADUATION   67

5. GERMANY   73

6. THE WORLD CHANGES   106

7. TURKEY   121

8. HER   138

9. TIME FLIES   148

10. THE GREAT ESCAPE   155

11. THE BOYS (AND GIRL) ARE BACK IN TOWN   164

12. AUF WIEDERSEHEN (GOODBYE)   173

13. BACK HOME (SORT OF)   180

14. HOME AGAIN (FOR NOW)   196

15. COLLEGE   202

16. THE BUREAU   214

17. THE LAUNCH PAD   232

18. THE END & THE BEGINNING   245

19. I'VE LOVED THESE DAYS   251

AFTERWORD   272

ACKNOWLEDGEMENTS   279

1
HOME

I was born in Norristown, Pennsylvania, in the early 70s. In 1704, a wealthy Quaker and close friend of William Penn by the name of Isaac Norris purchased the land that would later become known as Norristown. It became the county seat of Montgomery County in 1784 and was incorporated as a borough in 1812. Norristown is located along the Schuylkill River, just six miles from the border of Philadelphia. This meant that at birth, you were anointed as a Phillies, Eagles, Sixers, and Flyers fan. As I grew up in the seventies, we imitated the athletic abilities of stars like Ron Jaworski, Bill Bergey, Mike Schmidt, Steve Carlton, and the indomitable "Dr. J."

Of course, growing up just outside of Philadelphia meant that you not only worshipped Rocky Balboa, but also developed a healthy understanding of what it means to be an underdog and to fight for everything you get. I personally assimilated these ideals to such an extent that even today, forty-plus years later, a call to my cell phone is marked by the blasting trumpets of the Rocky theme song. Plain and simple, Norristown has historically been a blue-collar town, but it had its fair share of famous former residents, including baseball greats Tommy Lasorda, Mike Piazza, and Christian Walker, NFL quarterback Steve Bono, and actors Peter Boyle and Maria Bello. The town's population has consistently hovered around 35,000, and as I grew up in the area, it seemed that half of the town was Italian and the other half was Black. The city itself is divided into four distinct areas: the East End, the West End, the North End, and Downtown.

My family and I lived in the West End on Stanbridge Street, just a few blocks from the gothic red brick buildings of the Norristown State Hospital, which opened in 1876 as the State Lunatic Hospital at Norristown. Here, psychiatric patients, including the criminally insane, were housed and treated. Depending on their level of risk and abilities, some were permitted to leave the confines of the hospital. As such, it was not uncommon to see higher-functioning mentally ill residents of the State Hospital meandering down Stanbridge or Sterigere Streets. On at least one occasion, my mother came to check on me as I played on the sidewalk in front of our house, only to find that I had made a new playmate. To my recollection, the patient's name was John, who had bright white hair that vaguely resembled an aging pompadour. Rumor had it that he was once a police officer who experienced profound mental distress after shooting a child while on the job. John and I sat and played on the sidewalk until my mom came to investigate, at which point John continued on his walking tour of the town. It was also not uncommon to have residents of the State Hospital at our little league baseball games, especially since several of our fields were located on the grounds of the hospital. Of particular prominence was Raymond, who cheered loudly, but his jubilation was often drowned out by the sight of the tobacco juice that constantly dribbled from his lower lip and congealed on his white T-shirt. Still, Raymond's enthusiasm was routinely rewarded with an ice cream handed out to the players by a parent after the games. There, standing along the bleachers, Raymond would smile, eat his ice cream, and add a new stain to his shirt. It seemed as if the State Hospital residents were simply another fixture of the community, as they frequented Al's Cold Cuts or wandered outside DiRenzo's Tavern.

My childhood home was a 2,100-square-foot, three-story duplex that shared a common wall with our neighbors. These duplexes lined the north side of Stanbridge Street for block after block, with each set separated by about twenty feet of space. Within this space were two sidewalks leading to the rear of each neighboring house. Our backyard was lined by a row of hedges on each side, leaving a yard approximately 25 feet wide by 50 feet long. With such a narrow yard, all wiffle ball games required the batter to become very adept at hitting the ball straight up the middle. Failure to do so meant that the batter had to personally retrieve their foul ball from one of the numerous neighboring yards, a feat that could require jumping a chain-link fence, outsmarting a neighbor's dog, or plucking the errant ball from under a rose bush without a persnickety elderly neighbor taking notice. At the end of our yard were three concrete steps that led to a raised parking area, allowing my family to avoid parking in the alley separating our row of homes from the matching rows of homes on Noble Street just to the north. This same layout continued for block after block, street after street. I can honestly say that it was not until I first brought my wife to my house that I realized I lived in a city. Since we did not live in Philadelphia, I assumed we lived in the suburbs. This assumption was quickly corrected when I brought the

Midwesterner who would eventually become my wife to my boyhood home.

The alleyway that ran between blocks was a cornerstone of my childhood play. Here we reenacted grudge matches between the Eagles and Cowboys with our slowly deteriorating Nerf footballs. This is where we rode our bikes with extra care to avoid inconvenient potholes. This is where we had long tosses with our baseballs and gloves, silently hoping we didn't miss the ball and have to chase it down the gentle slope to intersecting Oak Street. Regardless of the game, there were always certain rules. The ball could not bounce off Mrs. Manning's garage door or it would be ruled foul. If the ball hit the pair of sneakers tied together by their shoelaces and hanging from the telephone wire, it would be considered dead. After all, without rules, life would be chaos. Despite our best efforts, every game eventually ended in chaos anyway, with a group of young burgeoning attorneys heatedly arguing their points before a non-existent judge. We would then head back to our respective residences with our noses out of joint until the next day when it would start all over again.

***

I was fortunate enough to grow up in a home with both parents present. My mother grew up in a small coal mining town named Jerome in western Pennsylvania. She was the ninth of ten children, and her upbringing in a town of roughly 400 people was frequently the basis of many stories throughout the years. We were told about how the mothers of the day battled the coal dust that caked the town and how my grandmother would bake bread daily on a cast-iron stove. We heard stories about how the townspeople lined the street as a bus dropped off a soldier in uniform, all silently hoping that it would be their son returning from Vietnam. We heard stories of kids sneaking out to have potato roasts and of my aunt falling ill after toppling into the river of waste that ran along the town, which was unceremoniously referred to as "the stink ditch." I remember being particularly fascinated by the stories of my Uncle Kenny, who was one of the U.S. Army's first Green Berets and was actually presented his beret by President Kennedy. In total, these stories were all held together by a palpable love shared by a coal miner and his wife, then passed down to and among their many children. It was, in many ways, the story of The Waltons before this beloved television show was ever created.

My father's upbringing, on the other hand, was the photo negative of my mother's. Growing up hundreds of miles to the east in Trooper, Pennsylvania, my father was a farm boy and one of three children born to his mother and father, though the couple was never actually married. His father was a baker by trade, but he seemed to excel more in drinking, carousing, and treating others poorly. Unlike my mother's childhood stories, my father's revolved around anecdotes of his father throwing bottles and pitchforks at him or sitting my dad on the bar as a toddler so that my grandfather could continue drinking. My dad recounted stories of driving with his father and the car breaking down; he would then order my dad to walk miles back to their home and drive another equally unsound vehicle on their property back to him. While these demands would shock the conscience of any parent today, they were made even worse by the fact that my father was only ten years old at the time. My dad also shared tales of his father mistreating his half-brother and forcing him to live in the woods behind the house after an argument. My father, always soft-hearted, would sneak food out to his half-brother when no one was looking.

Perhaps my favorite story about my paternal grandfather, who died long before I was born, revolves around a gifted alligator. Somewhere along the line, someone had given my grandfather a baby alligator. Living an unkempt lifestyle in the country, my grandfather allowed the alligator to roam free throughout the home. As alligators tend to do, the creature continued to grow. During a visit to my grandfather's home, my mother noticed the size of the reptile and strategically avoided placing her feet on the floor while seated. As common sense took over, my parents strongly encouraged my grandfather to get rid of the beast. He responded with his typical noncommittal promise to do so. Some weeks later, my father, an avid newspaper reader, was astounded to read a story about two young boys who found an alligator in Stony Creek near Trooper, Pennsylvania. Given that Pennsylvania is not known for such reptilian predators, my dad understandably accused his father of dumping the creature in the creek behind his home. Gruffly, his dad responded, "That's not my goddamn alligator." I'm sure it was just a strong coincidence that two alligators happened to reside in the small town of Trooper at the same time.

To escape such a difficult environment, my father decided to join the Marine Corps during the Korean War. He was quickly shipped off to Japan, where he was trained as an aerial radio operator. It soon became apparent that this may not have been the best use of the Marine Corps' resources, as my father repeatedly got airsick and was unable to complete his assigned duties. Luckily for him, his athletic prowess quickly got him reassigned to the camp's baseball team, and so he spent the majority of his three-year commitment diving for line drives instead of diving for airsick bags aboard a military aircraft.

Though clearly not raised in a religious family, my father accepted Jesus as his Lord and Savior while serving overseas and became a devout Lutheran from that day forward. Among his daily prayers was a personal plea that the Lord would find him a wife. My father returned to the Philadelphia suburbs after his service, and my mother moved to the area as a teenager after the death of her father from the coal miner's affliction known as black lung disease. Whether it was God's response to my father's incessant prayers or merely cosmic luck resulting from shared mutual friends, my parents were introduced. Shortly thereafter, and thanks to a secret ride to Elkton, Maryland, my parents eloped. My father was 24, and my mother was a 17-year-old high school senior. Unlike weddings in the modern age, it proved to be a relatively inexpensive day. Joining these two lives together cost a grand total of five dollars for the marriage license.

They then drove back home but kept the clandestine union hidden for several months before finally informing my maternal grandmother of their secret. Fortunately, my grandmother loved her newest son-in-law and was glad to have her ninth of ten children successfully married. Still, the attraction between my parents remains a mystery even today. While my father has often claimed that Juliana was the answer to his prayers, he sometimes jokes that the young 17-year-old from Jerome was simply looking for someone who could buy her cigarettes. Perhaps the truth is somewhere in between. One thing is for certain, however: on a near weekly basis, at the ages of 91 and 84, my dad will still put his arm around my mom and say, "Julie, if I had it to do all over again, I'd ask you to marry me." The seeming tenderness of the moment is always quickly broken by my mom's pat answer: "And I would say 'No.'" Again, was it God or pure luck?

***

The first child to come along was my sister, Robin. Three years later came Mandy, and slightly more than a year after that, my brother Drew. My mother then went through an additional four pregnancies, all of which ended in miscarriages, and a fifth pregnancy that resulted in the birth of a stillborn daughter they named Victoria. My father immediately had her buried in a tiny grave in neighboring Jeffersonville.

After eight years of devastating pregnancies, I was born. Since all of the neighbors were aware of my mother's difficulty in having additional children, my birth was considered a bit of a miracle, or at least a cause for shared neighborhood excitement. In fact, my sisters would often go out to play, but not before giving strict instructions that my mother was to call for them when I was getting a bath so they and their neighborhood friends could watch. Thankfully, this is not a tradition that has carried on into my adulthood... much to the relief of my current neighbors.

Three years after me came the fifth and final child, Eric. With such a large gap between me and the next oldest child, my father often referred to Robin, Mandy, and Drew as the 'first family' and Eric and me as the 'second family.' The distance between the 'two families' was magnified by the fact that my sister Robin married her husband Mike when she was only nineteen. This meant that not only were Eric and I ring bearers at their wedding, but we also had a brother-in-law by the ages of four and seven, respectively. After nearly 45 years of marriage, Eric and I have known Mike for practically all of our lives. To demonstrate this fact, Mike often tells the story of when he and Robin were newly married. He was approached while carrying Eric around a local store. A female patron asked if Eric was Mike's son, to which Mike laughed and rightfully identified the small child in his arms as his brother-in-law.

When I was ten, I lost my second sister, Mandy, to marriage. She too married a man named Mike. Apparently, between 1978 and 1981, the Philadelphia area was running short on groom's names. Due to the substantial age differences, both Mandy and Robin were like second and third mothers to me, and their respective Mikes became additional father figures. Their homes became frequent weekend getaways. This continued as they started their own families, and I readily embraced my new role as an uncle, a position I assumed at the mere age of ten.

My own childhood was wonderful. I had a mother who cooked, cleaned, and packed our lunches. She'd surprise us with special desserts like cream puffs or the culinary treat from western Pennsylvania known as the 'gob,' which is referred to elsewhere as the 'whoopie pie.' During the summers, she would hang sheets over the clothesline to create a tent from which Eric, the neighborhood kids, and I could launch secret missions against enemy armies comprised of other neighborhood kids. On particularly hot days, she would hang the garden hose over the clothesline, allowing us to run through it or play carwash with our bicycles.

I also had a father who was always ready to spend time with us. He would walk us to the corner store for a cherry coke and a pack of crackers. He would take us to the nearby Elmwood Park Zoo or to one of many neighborhood baseball fields for batting practice and ground balls. At Christmas time, he would take us on the local SEPTA train to Center City Philadelphia to see the Christmas light show at Wanamaker's Department Store. Perhaps my favorite outing was when he drove us to John James Audubon's first home in the United States in nearby Mill Grove. There, we would explore the historic home and admire Audubon's many pictures of birds and the various taxidermied animals that had been found in the surrounding woods. Still, it was our walks through the woods that I loved most. While my father strolled along, whistling a tune to himself, I always made it a point to run ahead, hide behind a tree, and jump out to scare him. It was a ritual that never proved successful, but continued nonetheless.

For many in the greater Philadelphia area, summer vacations meant a trip to the Jersey Shore. This yearly familial pilgrimage to Ocean City or Sea Isle City ranked just below Christmas in excitement. The days spent playing on the beach, body surfing, or fully extending into a wave to catch a ball like Harold Carmichael into the end zone at Vet Stadium were the epitome of childhood fun for Philly kids. For one week each year, my family would pile into the car and make the hellacious and seemingly endless drive to the South Jersey shore points. In reality, the trip was about an hour and a half, but for a kid bursting with excitement, it felt like driving across the country. We all felt a certain air of superiority as we drove in on Saturday morning, passing all the poor, sad souls driving in the opposite direction, mourning the end of their vacation. Surely, we would never share in that sense of loss and desperation. And yet, every year, six short but glorious days after our triumphant arrival in Ocean City, we too would hang our heads and drive back toward Philadelphia as we passed the next batch of lucky yet unsuspecting families driving in. For me, this return trip always felt like the end of all enjoyment, at least until Saint Nick promised to make an appearance approximately half a year later.

I truly loved being a kid. I loved playing baseball, football, and indoor soccer. I loved playing basketball, wiffle ball, and two-hand touch in our backyard and alley. I especially loved the games of war that we played. The best days were when all the kids from the neighborhood participated. The large group would split into two teams, slowly stalking the enemy from home to home up and down the block. Unlike today, with the extensive arsenal of Nerf guns available on the market, we were a lower middle-class neighborhood. This meant our 'guns' were often sticks or clothespins stuck together to create a handle and barrel. It was not the guns that made the game, but rather the hours-long chase throughout the neighborhood. There were no Nerf bullets or paintball projectiles to announce the start of an attack; instead, we relied on the dreaded verbal onslaught of "pow, pow, pow." A direct hit was marked by shouts of "I got you!" Not-so-direct hits resulted in well-reasoned arguments that vacillated between "No, you didn't" and "Yes, I did." Eventually, this cognitive jujitsu was resolved when the victim fell to the ground and counted to "seven Mississippi" while the shooter dashed toward their next ambush point.

Ambushes were a complicated mixture of brilliance and deception. I seemed to excel at this particular skill, positioning one of my shoes to stick out from a corner, making it seem as if I was doing a poor job of hiding from a small band of marauders sneaking between houses in my direction. As they attempted to launch their own sneak attack around the building, they would be met with a lonely shoe and a scream of "pow, pow, pow" from the opposite direction. This same misdirection could be accomplished by sticking my baseball hat in a bush or on the concrete ledge of the porch to make it appear as if I were crouching down in wait. This type of diabolical cat-and-mouse treachery continued until we were all eventually called in for dinner.

It's hard to get around the simple fact that I loved being a kid and I loved playing. In fact, I still remember the day I realized my childhood days of folly were coming to a close. I recall excusing myself from my younger brother, walking into our tiny half bath, taking a seat on the floor between the wall and the toilet, and crying as if my heart were broken. Being three years younger and probably feeling abandoned by my epiphany of impending adulthood, my brother yelled at me many times in subsequent years, asking rhetorically why I had to grow up. But despite my best efforts, the carefree days of early adolescence quickly faded into the teenage years. It was during this time that my family experienced a cataclysmic event that would drastically impact all our lives.

***

In the simplest terms, my family was never well-heeled. Both of my parents came from very poor backgrounds, and we grew up in a town of blue-collar workers. This combination meant we never had a lot of money. But when you live among others of the same socioeconomic status, your lifestyle seems normal. We were by no means poor; we just didn't have the extras cherished by many kids today. We had one television in the living room, which meant we all watched TV together. Because our house was built in the early 1900s, we had no central air conditioning. This meant my siblings and I spent countless evenings stuck to our bedsheets with the windows open, hoping for a breeze that never came. At times, we had a box fan in the window, but this only seemed to anger the warm summer air and blow it into the room like an inconsiderate hair dryer. I can still remember my mother's sage advice directing my brother and me to turn the fan around so that it would suck all the warm air out. I can assure you, there was no hidden stash of cool air waiting to replace the stifling air that was supposed to be vacated in her masterful plan. And so, you simply flipped and flopped on your twin bed like a fish on asphalt until you eventually fell asleep.

We did not go out to dinner like kids do today. Occasionally, we would get McDonald's, but that was the extent of our fine dining. In fact, we rarely ordered pizza. Instead, my mom would put frozen Ellio's pizza in the oven for a special treat. In a desperate attempt to get take-out pizza, I can remember hatching a surefire plan that was bound to bring a hot pie right to our dinner table. Somewhere along the line, I must have learned that a signed contract was legally binding. So, I sat down and wrote out a list of rules for a new game that Eric and I had supposedly created. I then informed my father that to make the rules official, we would need a parent to sign the document as a witness. Little did my unsuspecting father know that, buried within the fine print of the new rules, were the words "Brad and Eric get pizza tonight." While my plan was clearly brushing up against white-collar criminal fraud, I nonetheless found it to be a stroke of absolute brilliance. Unfortunately, I made the mistake of giving it to the wrong parent. My father has always been a voracious reader—books, newspapers, the Reader's Digest... the man read everything. Not surprisingly, he quickly located my secret clause and stated unambiguously, "No, Brad and Eric won't be getting pizza tonight." I then quickly realized that I should have given the document to my mother; she never read anything.

Our lack of wealth can also be demonstrated by many of the cars we had in our family. For example, my sister Robin's first car was an early sixties model Dodge Dart that my father bought for her from a neighbor for $75. The car was black—at least, the spray paint covering it was black. But the defining feature of this fine automobile was that it had a hole in the rear floorboards on the driver's side. This unique design meant that you could watch the road pass by while driving, similar to tourists in the Caribbean watching fish swim under a glass-bottomed boat. Luckily, my parents had outfitted this muscle car with a piece of plywood to cover the hole. It was a fix consistent with the safety standards of the mid-seventies. Always concerned for the well-being of her children, my mother would remind Robin as she drove off with me in tow (minus a car seat) to make sure that the hole was covered so that I didn't fall out. As I write about this now, I realize that I have been spending way too much on Mother's Day gifts over the years.

My first car, when I got my license in 1987, was not far off from Robin's spray-painted black beauty. It was a 1973 Dodge Dart sedan in beautiful Army green. Apparently, Dodge Darts grew on trees in Norristown back then. I remember driving with my dad when he saw it sitting at a gas station on Germantown Pike with a "For Sale" sign in the window. My dad pulled in to inquire about the vehicle, and $900 later, it was mine. For some unknown reason, I named the vehicle 'Hendley' after James Garner's character in the 1963 film *The Great Escape*. I was so profoundly grateful for my dad's generosity that I must have washed Hendley ten times before I even got my license. The vehicle was such a relic that it only had a lap belt instead of a shoulder seat belt. The high-beam headlight switch was a small button on the floor, and the previous owner had installed an FM converter so that the driver was not beholden to the AM radio that came from the factory. Still, Hendley was mine, and I loved her. Even though I routinely had to pop the hood and use a screwdriver to hold open the butterfly on the carburetor to get her running, she was all mine, and I was grateful to have a car.

Ultimately, my siblings and I developed an underlying gratitude for what we were given because we were not always given a lot, and certainly not the best. My dad routinely worked two or three jobs to provide for his children. To better himself and ultimately increase his earning potential, he worked his way through night school and obtained a Bachelor's Degree from Ursinus College in nearby Collegeville. It was an accomplishment nine years in the making. His diligence paid off, and the once forklift driver became an office worker. Even then, the money did not come rolling in. At that time, my parents could only afford one dress shirt for my father. This meant that every day after work, my mother would dutifully wash his shirt, iron it, and place it on a hanger for my dad's next day of work. However, my father's nose-to-the-grindstone approach to bettering himself eventually paid dividends, and he became an accountant with a manufacturing company in Northeast Philadelphia. His rise continued as he eventually became the company's Treasurer. Unfortunately, as often happens with businesses, the company was sold, and my father soon found himself out of a job.

Out of a sense of uncertainty and desperation, my dad made a drastic change in 1985. He decided to open a muffler shop and gas station in Hatfield, Pennsylvania, with the father of my Little League football teammate. My dad was set to handle the financial aspects of the business while my teammate's father was to run the actual muffler work. It was a decision that was completely out of character for my parents, but it was an exciting time, and I can remember being pulled out of school in the 8th grade for the grand opening of the business. I felt a bit like royalty. My father was going to own a business, and we were present on the ground floor to see what was about to be created.

Unfortunately, this excitement and anticipation were short-lived. Due to personality conflicts and various other factors, an attorney recommended that my father and his partner dissolve the partnership and file for personal bankruptcy. The business lasted only eight months. While my parents always struggled with money, this situation devastated them financially and emotionally. Creditors began calling, cars were repossessed in the middle of the night, and my mother cried. I can still remember my parents summoning my younger brother and me to the kitchen table. As we sat down, something immediately seemed out of the ordinary, as we certainly were not a family prone to family meetings. While I was not old enough to understand everything that was going on with my parents, I was certainly old enough to know that the situation was dire. Although the exact discussion has long faded from memory, the only words I can recall are, "We have no money left... but we will always love you."

***

In my opinion, one of the most underused—and perhaps most under-taught—concepts in current American culture is 'resilience.' While I was obviously scared to hear that my parents were now destitute, I felt a significant degree of comfort from the last part of their announcement. I never doubted that we would be okay. My parents were always hard workers, and I naturally assumed they would dig themselves—and us—out of this hole. And that is exactly what happened. My mom had multiple part-time jobs, and my dad immediately found work through a temporary service with Fidelity Bank in Philadelphia. Later, he found full-time employment with a concrete manufacturer that lasted for nearly 30 years. He also took on multiple part-time jobs as the digging continued.

It seemed that everyone knew of my parents' bankruptcy, and the outpouring of support was quite moving. The woman and fellow church member who owned the craft store where my mother worked part-time gave her a brown paper bag filled with money with strict instructions that it was not to be paid back, and my mother cried. Our neighbor, a small business owner, walked down the block and gave my parents three blank checks, telling them to make the checks out for whatever they needed. Again, my mother cried. Day by day, dollar by dollar, year after year, my parents worked to rebuild their lives. I watched as my mother kept a little notebook in which she documented every payment of every bill as they struggled to right the ship. Meticulously, she kept track of the money they owed friends and family who were gracious enough to loan them money until everyone—even her boss at the craft store—was paid back in full. Their honor, their self-respect, and their hard work left an indelible mark on my life. So too did their struggle, which I subconsciously hoped to never repeat.

2

ENLISTMENT

Growing up in Norristown, you generally had one of two options for high school: Norristown Area High School (NAHS) or the Catholic high school, Bishop Kenrick. The children in my family all went to Norristown. For the majority of us kids, graduating as a Norristown Eagle marked the end of our academic progression. Despite my father's nine-year blood-and-guts pursuit of a bachelor's degree and the obvious benefit he derived from this undertaking, advanced education was not a priority in my family, and certainly not an expectation. To this day, I am uncertain whether this was unique to my family or symptomatic of our blue-collar neighborhood. Perhaps it was a combination of both.

My oldest sister, Robin, successfully earned an associate's degree from the nearby Montgomery County Community College, more colloquially known as 'MONTCO.' My sister Mandy, on the other hand, immediately landed an office job. My brother Drew was another story. We used to tease him frequently about his... intellectual nonconformity. A prime example of this shortcoming can easily be observed in his response to a friend's terrible accident. Drew was made aware of the seriousness of the accident and was informed that his friend was so profoundly injured that he had lost all motor skills. Drew replied with the foolish question, "Oh man, you mean he can't drive?" Still, what Drew lacked in intellectualism, he made up for with athleticism.

He was a tremendous baseball player and was drafted by the Milwaukee Brewers out of high school in 1981. My father's excitement about this event was palpable. While some might think that such remarkable athletic ability would spark jealousy in a younger brother, the eight-year age difference between us precluded any animosity. Instead, I remember Drew calling home from preseason training in Arizona to update my parents on his progress. I can also recall answering the phone and asking him if he had met any famous players, with him promising to send home batting gloves or other baseball paraphernalia for me to enjoy. Unfortunately, the excitement in our home quickly faded when my brother was released by the Brewers organization a short while later. The phone call in which my dad received this news was the first time I had ever heard him use a curse word. Even then, all he could muster was the word "jackass."

My brother returned to Norristown and continued playing with various teams in and around the area. I don't know what it is about Norristown, but the area seemed unusually gifted with athletes at that time, particularly baseball players. Not only was my brother recruited by a major league baseball team, but so were many of his friends. Perhaps there was something in the water of the Schuylkill River. Maybe it was because Latshaw Field sits not only curiously close to the center of town, but also served as the hub of life for many fans of Norristown sports teams. In those days, the lights of Latshaw Field shone brightly on the field as amateur baseball players from the 18-and-older Perkiomen Valley

Twilight League battled for area dominance. No team was more dominant at that time than my brother's team, the Norristown A's. He and his teammates, many of whom also had short stints with major league organizations, competed in a league that could easily be considered semi-pro. People crowded the bleachers along the first and third base dugouts, as well as the hill that ran along right and center fields. From their perches, fans watched these summer evening battles while kids playing along the adjacent Stony Creek plucked foul balls from its shallow waters and quickly returned them to the umpires.

Because I knew most of Drew's friends and teammates, I was often granted permission to sit in the team's dugout as I became a teenager. This felt like being granted a backstage pass to a concert, and I often felt the admiration of my friends as I entered. I was incredibly proud of my older brother, and he would often allow me to tag along. We would play basketball in our parking area, where he would delight in defeating his younger and much shorter brother. He would serve as the steady quarterback in one-on-one games between me and the neighbor, a position where he could exert the least amount of energy possible. There were times when, out of the blue, he would ask if I wanted to make a fast-food run with him, or he would let me sleep on the floor of his bedroom on sweltering summer nights after he finally broke down and bought himself a window air conditioner. As a ballplayer in the eighties, he dipped tobacco, much to the displeasure of my parents. At times, he even allowed me to partake in this nasty habit by overseeing me as I put a pinch of Skoal between my cheek and gum. Then, ten minutes later, he would direct me to run inside, thoroughly rinse my mouth out, and, most importantly, hide this delinquency from my mother.

While we were close and I looked up to my older brother, it was painfully clear that I would never be the athlete he was. This meant that when both of us had ballgames on the same night, parental interest favored my brother. Even as an adolescent, this seemed more logical to me than hurtful. It only made sense for my folks to watch the better athlete playing more competitive baseball. Despite the rationality of this decision-making, growing up in my brother's shadow led to two clear realizations. First, I would have to find a way to compete with him at something other than baseball. Second, I would have to work twice as hard at whatever I decided to do.

The one area where I knew I could surpass my brother was in scholastic achievement. While I cannot say that I enjoyed my time in the public school system, I certainly took it seriously. I was always a strong studier, and my grades reflected that effort. Most of my grades were A's, some were B's, and thanks to a ridiculously difficult chemistry teacher, one grade was a C. My C was an incredible accomplishment, as my classmates and I often considered a test grade of 20% to be a magnificent success in that particular class. This includes my fellow student who went on to become an accomplished pediatrician in Philadelphia. Still, through a great deal of hard work, horrendous stress, and a tutor, I was successful in eking out the lowest grade of my academic career. Clearly, success comes in many forms.

As my high school years continued, my grades remained high, and I ended up graduating in the top handful of students in my class of over 300. One would think that my academics would have easily put me on a college trajectory, but this did not prove to be the case. Unlike modern parents, my folks had no experience in preparing children for college. There were no discussions about post-high school plans, no push to research schools, and certainly no college tours. This is not meant to cast any blame on my parents; it was simply a language they were not familiar with. As the fourth of five children, none of my older siblings attended a four-year university, leaving me with no footsteps to follow in and no template to tap into. For my family, understanding and negotiating this process was like expecting a member of a reclusive tribe in the Congo to comprehend the intricate rules of professional football.

In addition to having no experience with college, I also had no motivation. By the start of my senior year of high school, I had had enough of schooling and definitely had no appetite for university life. Beyond that conclusion, I had no idea what I wanted to do. Then, an Army recruiter came to our school. As I mentioned, my father was a Marine during the Korean War, my uncle and two of my cousins served in the Army and Marine Corps during the Vietnam War, and my brother-in-law was in the Air Force during the early seventies. While I would not consider us a military family, I certainly had family members who served. Obviously, this had some influence on me. Still, the influence of popular culture in the United States at that time cannot be overlooked either.

By the time I entered my teens in the mid-1980s, movies and television often seemed to follow three significant plotlines. Given that the U.S. was approaching the 20-year anniversary of the height of the Vietnam War, Hollywood was not lacking in its demonstration of nostalgia. Films like Full Metal Jacket, Platoon, Hamburger Hill, Uncommon Valor, Born on the Fourth of July, and Good Morning Vietnam, along with television shows like China Beach and Tour of Duty, kept the Vietnam War at the forefront of the American consciousness. I watched them all. America's involvement in the ongoing Cold War was also prevalent in the minds of moviegoers, portrayed through a slew of films in which the evil Soviet Union stood in stark contrast to the goodness and heroism of brave American protagonists. Movies such as Rambo II, Rambo III, Rocky IV, The Hunt for Red October, Firefox, Spies Like Us, and even Top Gun fueled the anti-Soviet mentality as Americans battled their Russian enemies on the screens of movie theaters. Of particular note, especially for me and many friends, was the film Red Dawn, in which high school students band together under their school nickname, "the Wolverines," to fight back against invading Soviet and Cuban soldiers. At 13 years old, this movie, above all others, activated the part of my brain responsible for motivating young men to protect their families and homeland.

In addition to these two overarching themes, Hollywood in the 1980s also witnessed the rise of testosterone-filled action stars like Arnold Schwarzenegger, Sylvester Stallone, Chuck Norris, Jean-Claude Van Damme, Steven Seagal, Mel Gibson, and Bruce Willis. Two aspects of this unique period in Hollywood are particularly interesting: 1) these heroes were typically portrayed as unabashedly "good guys," and 2) they were unapologetic males. Other than perhaps Dwayne "The Rock" Johnson, this type of action star has long since been replaced by beautiful and petite women who swiftly dispatch multiple men three times their size. Additionally, productions like The Sopranos, Breaking Bad, Dexter, Ozark, the numerous Star Wars reboots chronicling the rise of Darth Vader, and the inexplicable television series Lucifer have left audiences begrudgingly rooting for the bad guys. As a result of these creative developments, it appears that young males today who have a penchant for goodness and heroism are often left wanting.

This was not the case for many young men growing up in the U.S. in the 1980s. Fueled by a steady diet of these films and action stars, along with the values instilled in me by my parents, I found myself bolstered by feelings of goodness, strength, justice, love of the military, and, of course, patriotism. It is therefore no surprise that when the Army recruiter arrived at our school, I was drawn to him. We talked, and he informed me about what the Army had to offer. My interest was piqued, and the wheels in my mind began turning. Later, I visited the recruiting office in Norristown and gathered additional information about the Army. For me, the decision was made. All that remained was a discussion with my parents.

***

Many of my important conversations with my parents took place at the kitchen table, so I decided this would be the perfect venue for such a life-changing discussion. As we sat eating dinner, I broached the subject in an ambush fashion.

"I decided to join the Army," I said between mouthfuls.

As if choreographed, my parents' jaws dropped slightly as they both looked in my direction. This hand grenade of an announcement led to a myriad of questions about how and when I came to this decision. I explained my conversations with the recruiter, my disinterest in college, and my desire to serve our country. I continued to build my case by highlighting the advantages of military service as presented by the recruiter. Just as there was no precedent among the children of my family for applying to a four-year university, there was also no existing model for joining the military. I was treading on virgin soil as far as my family was concerned. Though shocked by my announcement, neither parent expressed any negative opinions. Coming from a patriotic Christian family living in a blue-collar suburb of Philadelphia, military service was not an illogical or deplorable life plan. Arrangements were then made for the three of us to have a sit-down with the Army recruiter so my parents could have their lingering questions answered.

Whether it was teenage impetuousness or my inherent tendency to simply go for it, I entered the recruiter's office with full confidence that I would retire from the U.S. Army. As my parents and I sat on the business side of the recruiter's desk, we began to discuss my interests regarding a military occupational specialty. The majority of my childhood had been spent playing baseball, football, soccer, and even a couple of seasons of basketball, although my height and talent level did not allow for additional years of shooting hoops. As I became a teenager, I also began to work out and exercise religiously. For me, there was only one option: Infantry.

According to the Army's own promotional materials, "The infantry is the main land combat force and backbone of the Army. Infantrymen are responsible for defending our country against any threat by land, as well as capturing, destroying, and repelling enemy ground forces." To me, any other specialty was a copout. If I was going to do this, I wanted to be part of the backbone. I wanted to take pride in what I did for the Army. I didn't want to push paper or guard a facility; I wanted to defend our nation. In my mind, that is what true patriots do, and I was ready to go. So certain was I of this decision that I was mentally prepared to sign up for a 20-year commitment, not that any such commitment officially exists. Thankfully, my parents were a little more measured in their approach to my newfound decision. Once I expressed my interest in becoming an Infantryman, the recruiter mentioned that the Army was offering an enlistment special of two years and fourteen weeks for recruits looking to join the infantry. This accounted for Basic Training, Advanced Individualized Training, and then a two-year commitment.

If I could not enlist for a straight 20 years, I was willing to compromise with a 4-year enlistment. Still, my parents broke it down for me into a very simplistic, yet incredibly intuitive, mathematical formula: two years is a lot less than four years if the Army proved not to be my cup of tea. And so, with an assurance from the recruiter that I could always extend my enlistment in the future, I agreed to this two-year option. The recruiter explained to us that the Army's Infantry School is located at Fort Benning, Georgia, where I would be trained to be an Infantryman. He assured my mother that, since I was only enlisting for two years, I was unlikely to be stationed overseas and would instead spend the entirety of this initial enlistment period at Fort Benning. Being only seventeen at the time, my parents signed the necessary paperwork for me to enter the Army's Delayed Enlistment Program, allowing me to complete my high school education before starting Basic Training. With all of our signatures, the deal was done, and my plan for the future was set.

On October 25, 1988, my recruiter drove me to the Military Examinee Processing Station in Philadelphia, where I filled out an ungodly amount of paperwork. In addition, I underwent a less-than-enjoyable group physical administered by what appeared to be a practicing mad scientist. At the end of the day, I was brought to a room with several other young military hopefuls from various branches. The floor was covered in green astroturf, and the walls were adorned with countless flags. This room had a distinctly different feel from the gray, disinteresting government offices I had traversed throughout the day. Something special seemed to take place in this room. An Army officer entered and asked each of us to raise our hands as we were jointly sworn into military service and vowed to support and defend the Constitution of our great nation. This proved to be a very inspirational moment in my young life, and I felt the weight of my commitment not only to the U.S. Army but also to the United States of America as I raised my right hand and repeated the words spoken to our group. After the brief ceremony, I received my orders: Basic Training at Fort Benning, Georgia, was set for August 30th, just a short ten months later.

3
FORT BENNING

I returned to high school a different person. Though it was only one day, I had already received a glimpse of military life during my trip to the MEPS station in Philadelphia. The decision had been made, and I felt a great deal of comfort in knowing for certain what my post-graduation plans were. I also returned from the recruiter's office that day with a gray t-shirt bearing the word 'Army' in black block letters. On some level, the gift from my recruiter was humorous. It reminded me of the t-shirts often found hanging in the small novelty shops lining the Ocean City Boardwalk, except mine had a small twist: "I signed my life away to the U.S. Army and all I got was this lousy t-shirt." Still, the gift fostered within me a sense of belonging and a purpose greater than my own personal pursuit of a college degree.

Parents and neighbors had questioned my decision. It was not uncommon for people to comment to my mother that my choice to join the Army seemed counterintuitive based on how smart they believed I was. Though well-meaning, it was an inherently rude question. Were they suggesting that my decision to serve my country made me stupid, or that only stupid people joined the military? Though the question occasionally ruffled my mother's feathers a bit, I remained unfazed. Something special was brewing in my future, and I was excited.

It is amusing now to think that I had been far more frightened to attend college than to join the military. My only concern about my impending enlistment was whether I would be able to handle the physical requirements, especially since I would be attending the Army's Infantry School. I therefore began an incessant regimen of lifting and running—running and lifting, and running, and running, and running. I was determined to make things hard now, so that they would be that much easier come August.

Unlike those high school students preparing for college, there were no major purchases for my parents to anticipate. There was no pre-college shopping spree necessary. I did not require a new comforter set, desk lamp, or storage organizers. My bare necessities, including not only my clothing but also my haircut, would be provided for me by the Army. However, there was one item I received from my parents that Christmas that proved to be a necessary and important gift.

The small box I opened on Christmas morning contained a silver necklace and medal bearing the Luther Rose. This particular Lutheran symbol dates back to the early 1500s. Though the necklace was completely silver in color, Martin Luther explained that the colored version featured a red heart containing a black cross in the center, designed to remind Lutherans that the righteous live by faith in Christ. The white rose, rather than a red rose, beneath the heart reflects the color of heavenly spirits and angels, while the rose itself signifies that faith in Christ brings joy, comfort, and peace. Beneath the white rose is a field of blue, representing the color of heaven and reminding us of the heavenly joy that awaits us at the end of this life. Lastly, a gold ring encircles the entire symbol, signifying the unending nature of our future lives in heaven. Perhaps even more notable were the words inscribed on the back of the medal: "I am a Lutheran."

As a devout Lutheran, my father ensured that the church played an important role in his children's lives. We were all baptized in the church, attended Catechism, were confirmed there, and participated in Sunday school. My mother helped make wreaths for the Christmas service and routinely hosted 'coffee hour' after the weekly services. She also helped prepare the large breakfasts after the Easter service, during which all the parishioners sat down and ate together.

My father served as a member of the church council, as an usher, and as the Sunday school treasurer. As a child, I would wait for him in the church office on Sundays while he collected and counted the offering receipts from the service and the Sunday school students. Many times, after church, he would take the flowers from the service and deliver them to parishioners in local hospitals. For many years, my parents even helped cut the grass and weed the flowerbeds at the church. As teenagers, we all served as acolytes, assisting the pastor during services. Rarely did we miss a Sunday of church. In fact, I can remember being sick one Sunday and my dad allowing me to stay home. At the time, it felt like I had won the lottery to actually miss a day of church and stay on the couch watching television instead.

My father's secret plan proved very effective for me. Spiritual muscle memory soon kicked in, and I found myself ushering and teaching Sunday school classes as a teenager while my faith blossomed. The Lutheran medal I received on that Christmas morning in 1988 was, therefore, a tremendously meaningful gift from my parents. It was a gift that I would carry into the Army as a reminder of not only where I came from but also who I am. I immediately placed the necklace around my neck, and I am proud to say that, 35 years later, it remains in place. So, while I did not require school supplies and dorm room sundries for my impending journey, I certainly felt loved and protected by both my family and my God. Ultimately, I called on both not long thereafter.

***

After months of preparing and waiting, August 29th finally arrived. I was awakened by my mother, who had taken a seat at the end of my bed and was now crying. In my excitement about this new phase of my life, it appeared I had underestimated the impact that my leaving was having on her. Some families say "I love you" at the drop of a hat; these few words mark the end of every phone call or accentuate the departure of every family member leaving home for school or work. Mine was not such a family. Rarely did we say these words to one another. Instead, the sentiment was easily and efficiently communicated through the things we did for one another and the time we spent together as a family. Still, to see my mother sobbing at the end of my bed spoke those words clearer than any Hallmark card could have offered at that moment. It was an uncharacteristically tender moment for us both, but it proved to be a punctuation mark for what could be considered the end of my childhood.

Later that day, I heard a quick blast from a car horn in front of my house. Dressed in a pair of jeans and a Doobie Brothers concert t-shirt (an outfit that I would come to know as 'civilian clothes' in just a few short hours), I hugged my parents goodbye, slung my small bag across my shoulder, and left through the front door. My mother took a picture before I left. I recently found this picture during our 'death cleaning.' The happiness and excitement on my face were immeasurable by any modern instrument of physiological science. Little did I know, as I made my way down the front steps to my recruiter's car, that those emotions would soon be thoroughly and completely obliterated.

***

The following evening, I found myself on a bus driving from the Atlanta Airport to Fort Benning. The bus was packed with other young men just like me. They hailed from towns all over the United States. Given that the majority of Norristown residents rarely seem to leave the confines of southeastern Pennsylvania, this was, in itself, an adventure. I quickly learned what would become the standard military icebreaker: "Where ya from?" It was a question that invited discussions about home, families, girlfriends, favorite sports teams, and a myriad of other important topics. And so, conversations continued excitedly as introductions were made and wisecracks were launched in various directions while our bus hurled toward Columbus, Georgia. As we entered Fort Benning, the already fevered pitch seemed to become more raucous. Finally, the motorcoach pulled in front of a low, flat reception station building and stopped. With a sense of cautious and quiet uncertainty, the demeanor of the bus came to a crashing halt precisely as the bus driver placed the vehicle in park.

As we all stared out the windows, the front door of the reception building opened. Out walked a man clad in his camouflage battle dress uniform (BDUs). Dressed in civilian clothing, we immediately noticed how his uniform set him apart from the occupants of our motorcoach. However, when he placed the 'Smokey the Bear' hat on his head, the difference between him and us became an insurmountable chasm. This unmistakable head covering marked our first sighting of a drill sergeant. The significance of this moment was met with a collective, breathless "Oh shit" from our group.

The drill sergeant strode confidently from the building to our bus. In those brief steps, every military movie I had ever seen battled for prominence in my memory, but the clear winner was Full Metal Jacket. The ethos surrounding the dreaded drill sergeant is well-known by both veterans and civilians alike. I had seen the movies; I knew what was coming. I was prepared. I just needed to wait out the storm.

With three large steps, the drill sergeant entered the cramped interior of the bus. "Good evening, gentlemen. Welcome to Fort Benning, the home of the United States Army Infantry."

With a smile, the drill sergeant greeted us with unexpected politeness and a sense of professional warmth. I quickly realized that the movies had been way off target. Hollywood had, yet again, overly dramatized the truth as a means of keeping moviegoers engrossed in their films. This experience was going to be very different from what I had anticipated.

After a few more words of introduction, the drill sergeant smiled again, and you could almost smell the pungent air of trepidation release from each of our bodies. Others were obviously feeling the same sense of relief that I was. As the drill sergeant finished his welcome speech, his final word hung in the air for just a second. Then it hit.

"Now you have exactly thirty seconds to get your asses off of my bus! Move! Move! Move!"

The warm welcome immediately dissolved into rage as the drill sergeant screamed obscenities that ricocheted around us. There was no dramatization in this scene. The drill sergeant was enraged as we bounced against each other like heated atoms, struggling to exit the bus door. The only words to describe the new interior of the bus were 'sheer panic.' As we pushed through the door, more drill sergeants assembled around us as if oozing from the walls like dark specters. They gathered and squawked like a flock of seagulls swarming handfuls of popcorn thrown from the beach. But instead of popcorn, this screaming group of men fed on the fear developing among the gaggle of new recruits. As we clamored to remove our bags from the storage area beneath the bus, drill sergeants got in the faces of civilian-clothed recruits struggling to hold back their panic and desperately suppress their tears. Some were unsuccessful in this fight, and their tears quickly drew the attention of more swarming drill sergeants. The weak received more and more unwanted attention as drill sergeants screamed in their faces about all the horrible things that awaited them and how their mothers were no longer there to help.

I quickly realized that survival meant staying off the radar. The key was to fade blissfully into the background while other lightning rods took the heat from the fuming and spitting drill sergeants. Like trying to collect a spilled grocery bag of ping pong balls, the drill sergeants eventually herded us into a formation where we stood in rows, equidistant from our fellow recruits. The remainder of the evening was a blur of screaming and commands as we were moved to the chow hall. Upon entering, we were directed to provide the last four digits of our social security numbers to the attendant. This was not an easy task for some. At eighteen years of age, some in the group had not yet memorized their social security numbers. This led to backups in the chow line, which, in turn, invited more screaming from the drill sergeants. These poor souls then found themselves in push-up position, or what the Army refers to as the "front-leaning rest position."

For those lucky enough to enter the chow hall unscathed, they were quickly informed that there was to be no talking from that point forward. They then marshaled us through the chow line as we expediently threw food onto our plates. Sitting down at the table, I was at least glad to have some food in front of me. Realizing time was likely of the essence, I took a forkful of food and directed it toward my mouth. However, before my fork reached my lips, the screaming started again.

"Everybody out! Chow's over! Move it! Move it!"

Without a single morsel of food hitting my mouth, I joined the others who scrambled to put up their trays and exit the chow hall. The only thing running through my mind at that moment was, "Oh my God. I'm going to starve to death in this place."

***

By the end of the evening, we were all placed into a large open bay with row upon row of industrial-looking beds. We stowed our meager belongings in the adjacent wall lockers, and the lights were turned out. As we lay there in the darkness and the silence enveloped us, occasional sobs and sniffles could be heard. It was like so many prison movies in which the 'new meat' arriving at the prison wept quietly in their cells as the reality and futility of their current situations smacked them square in the face. For me, thoughts raced through my tired yet overloaded mind. What the hell had I been thinking? Why would someone voluntarily do this to themselves? Maybe college wouldn't have been so scary after all. What would they have for breakfast, and would I actually get a chance to taste it this time? What was everyone doing at home right now? Round and round the thoughts swirled until I finally passed out, my mind a complicated mixture of exhaustion and fear.

The next day, and every day thereafter, began with the expansive rows of overhead fluorescent lights crackling to life. As if the darkness of 4:30 in the morning being pierced by such intrusive and blinding light was not awful enough, it brought with it a new round of screaming. Like hitting the pause button on a video, the same story from the night before sprang to life, and we were yelled at to hurry up and get dressed as yet more panic ensued. Intermittently, we were commanded to hit the floor and commence push-ups as drill sergeants paced up and down the aisles of beds, watching us beat our faces on the cold, clean floors. I could remember hating the sound of my alarm clock back home. How sheltered was I?

Finally dressed, we made our way downstairs, and with slightly more ease than the previous evening, grouped ourselves into formation. As we stood there, I came to detest our civilian clothing and uncut hair. Other companies that had arrived at Basic Training weeks before us marched past on their way to the chow hall. They wore their BDUs and marched with a precision that highlighted their meager seniority. In contrast, our civilian clothes and comparatively long hair announced our recent arrival at Fort Benning. Collectively, we were the lowest rung on the training ladder. All I could think about was how these slightly more experienced recruits must be snickering to themselves at the gawky and untamed newbies standing there, confused and afraid. I wondered if they felt superior to us or simply pitied us, thinking, "At least we're not those guys."

It's funny now that I think about it. Misery doesn't actually love company; what misery truly loves is someone who is even more miserable. As the new arrivals, we unknowingly took on the unenviable position of being the 'more miserable.' For that reason, I could not wait to be issued my uniforms and have my hair cut. While I may have been part of the more miserable group, I despised looking the part. I also could not wait to be assigned to my new training platoon. Since we had just arrived at reception, we were all in a holding pattern. Eventually, we would be divided into one of four platoons that would make up Bravo Company of the 2nd Battalion, 54th Infantry Regiment. But for now, we were stuck squarely in the administrative period. This was the purgatory that preceded hell. To me, the thought of spending a week in this transitional limbo was unbearable. It felt like being asked to sit in a waiting room for days, knowing that the next room involved a severe beating. The way I saw it, if I was going to be given a beating, I would just as soon have it done sooner rather than later.

My dreams were answered about a week later when I was assigned to 1st Platoon, along with 49 other hopefuls. Thus began the formation of my new Basic Training family. As I began to meet and learn about my new platoon mates, I quickly realized that the world is full of many different people. Some are friendly, and some are not. Some have crazy accents, and some do not. Some have been blessed with common sense, while others seem to have missed that particular gene sequence. This was made painfully clear to me when one of my new platoon mates picked up one of the tiny lizards that could be found running all around Fort Benning. Looking at the tiny creature, he popped it in his mouth, then began chewing it before opening wide for all of us to see. Whether it was for laughs, shock value, or simply to make the audience gag, I was quickly learning that people can be very different.

***

Despite our differences, I immediately had 49 brothers from all over the United States, each bringing their own personalities and unique sets of baggage. There was an Italian and a Puerto Rican from New York City whose accents were not immediately understood by the guys from the Deep

South. Not surprisingly, these Southern boys spoke with a twang that sounded completely unfamiliar to those of us from the East Coast. We had a Californian who talked and swaggered like a surfer. We even had three Eskimos who rarely spoke; when they did, they were hard to understand. Not only did these three men seem like they hailed from a foreign country, but their noses also bled routinely from the unfamiliar swampy climate of the southeastern United States. Apparently, we all had different things to adapt to.

Within our burgeoning family, there was also a Texan who I was fascinated to learn graduated from a high school class of only nine students. In my typical sarcastic manner, I commented that the odd number must have left someone short of a date on prom night. What was particularly interesting about this new brother from Texas was that he had never met a Black person before. Making this point to a Black soldier, he innocently asked if he could touch the soldier's hair. The soldier agreed, and the follicle analysis commenced. As I write about this today in our hyper-divided country, both of these young men seemed almost childlike in their approach to and understanding of one another. There was no Black, white, Hispanic, or Asian. We were all just green—green in our uniforms and green in our level of soldiering experience. Our combined success would ultimately depend on our ability to interact with one another as a group and as unique, sometimes quirky individuals.

Perhaps what our country is currently missing is a shared point of unification. For 1st Platoon, we had two such points. First, we all shared a desire to survive the mistake we made in coming to Fort Benning. Second, we all shared a hatred of our three drill sergeants. With their own unique personalities, our three emotionally abusive fathers seemed to delight in the fear they instilled in us. In those early days, there were only two means of communication: yelling and yelling louder. Like evil comic book villains, they each seemed to have their own personal superpower.

The senior drill instructor enjoyed psychological torture. From the outset, his favorite method of attack was to tell us that our Christmas leave would be canceled. Many of us were already regretting our career choice; completing our training in mid-December and returning home to our families for Christmas was all we had to look forward to. Obviously, he was aware of this fact and maniacally enjoyed dashing our hopes by telling us we would be shipped directly to our first duty stations without a Christmas break. As if this were not bad enough, he also took great pleasure in repeatedly telling those of us with girlfriends that our girls had already moved on and found new men to replace us. For some unknown reason, the name of this hopefully imaginary rival for our girlfriends' affection became known as "Jody." So, as we marched in cadence throughout the base, he would yell out rhymes about how Jody had taken our girls and gone. During mail call, the drill sergeant also liked to identify a letter from someone's girlfriend, hand it to the recipient, and then comment that she was probably writing to tell him she was leaving him for Jody. It was his way of bayoneting soldiers who were already wounded.

The other drill sergeant's superpower was his unique ability to create personal hurricanes. This power came to life whenever someone was foolish enough to leave his wall locker unlocked. Should someone be unlucky enough to make this mistake, they would likely return to find every single personal item they possessed strewn around the bay area where all fifty of us slept. As soon as we walked in to find a toothbrush, fingernail clippers, shampoo, letters from home, and pictures of loved ones scattered across the floor, we knew that "Hurricane Willie" had struck again. All we could do in those circumstances was pray that, when we returned to our bunks, our wall lockers would be safe and secure.

Our final drill sergeant was intimidating in his own right, mostly because he rarely spoke. He simply stared at you without actually seeing you. Unlike the other two, there was no clue or hint of what he was thinking. In fact, the only conversation I ever had with him occurred during physical training (PT) one morning. Unfortunately, in the middle of jumping jacks, bear crawls, and push-ups, my colon made it painfully clear that I was in immediate need of the bathroom. I stepped out of formation, approached the drill sergeant, and asked, "Drill Sergeant, I'm going to explode. Can I hit the head?"

Completely devoid of emotion, he asked, "You really need to go?"

As the intestinal gurgling continued and my panic increased, all I could muster in response was, "Yeah." As I said it, I immediately realized that in my haste, I not only failed to use the more formal version of "Yes," but I also neglected to end my answer with "Drill Sergeant." My silent hope that he had overlooked my verbal misstep was quickly eradicated.

"Yeah?" he repeated, incredulous.

I quickly corrected myself. "I mean yes, Drill Sergeant."

The man was not fooled. "Oh hell no. Get your ass back in formation."

Realizing how painfully close I had come to the sweet relief of a bathroom trip, I trotted back to my position, pinching, puckering, and praying that my gray PT shorts would not soon turn a rich shade of mahogany. Whether it was divine intervention or simply mind over sphincter, I was able to finish out the last few minutes of exercise before breaking the land speed record to the latrine.

***

And so it went for 14 weeks. We walked on eggshells, desperately hoping to avoid individualized attention from these three men, and we were incredibly thankful to those who received their attention routinely as it kept the heat off of the rest of us. The initial days were painful. In writing this story, I decided to peruse my letters to my parents from those dark days. The writing was sloppy and brief, as there was rarely any time to write. As a result, many of us would rush to scribble a simple note to our loved ones to at least let them know we were alive. With no cell phones, FaceTime, or social media apps, we relied on the postal service to provide updates and receive warm wishes and words of encouragement from home. Reading those early letters, I once again felt the emotional pain we all experienced. I also felt shame and regret over the worry I must have caused my parents during those early days of Basic Training.

Clearly, my story of homesickness, heartache, and despair was not unique. As I made friends among my platoon mates, others shared similar stories of loneliness, fear, and self-doubt. It became an area where we could all bond immediately. It was a form of group therapy, even though none of us understood what group therapy was. Unfortunately, not everyone was successful in their battle. One of our platoon members took a large handful of pills that he had received from the doctor in an attempt to end his life. Luckily, another soldier identified his strange behavior and reported it. He was quickly rushed to the hospital, and though he physically healed from his actions, he was labeled as dangerous and removed from our ranks. With a similar motive, another soldier reportedly tied the cord of a floor buffer around his neck and tried to throw the buffer out of the window. Fortunately, his ill-conceived plan was quickly thwarted. Sadly, not all suicide attempts were caught in time. Word reached our platoon that a recruit in another training company had walked onto the firing range, clicked his M-16 onto full auto, and shot himself in the mouth, instantly taking his own life. Each of us seemed to deal with this news in our own way. Our senior drill sergeant, on the other hand, glibly commented, "Well, that's one less recruit we have to train." It was yet another reminder of how different people can be.

Having put my letters to my parents in date order and reading through them 35 years later, I observed a clear and unmistakable pattern. It was a distinct upward trajectory ranging from despair to hopelessness to acceptance to confidence. Simply put, these letters reflected the undeniable process of resilience. At the age of 52, I realized exactly what the Army had been doing. They took fifty complete strangers, threw them together, and then physically and emotionally disassembled them until nothing but the core of their being remained. Then, systematically, they set about building us back up to something new—something stronger. But it was not easy, and it did not happen overnight.

Perhaps the most difficult part of the whole experience was the fact that you were never alone. You slept four feet away from guys on either side of you. When you woke up, they were still there. When you did PT, they were there. When you went to breakfast, lunch, and dinner, they were there. When you showered, shaved, brushed your teeth, and went to the bathroom, they were there. When you got a chance to call home for five minutes on the weekends, they were standing in line waiting for the phone with you. At the end of the day, when you shined your shoes or did your laundry, they were there. For those who lived their lives as party people, this meant they had a constant audience and plenty of ears to bend. For those like me, who were much more introverted, this meant you never had a chance to recharge your mental batteries. Sadly, for the first eight weeks, you were not permitted to have a Walkman, the distant ancestor of the iPod. This meant you couldn't even put on your headphones as you lay in bed in the dark to escape those permanently around you through music.

Yet, as time went by, the strangers they stuck you with weeks earlier slowly became family. Some were close brothers, while others were distant cousins you didn't necessarily care for but had to tolerate. We also began to learn how to cheat the system and push the boundaries within the game rules that were laid out. For example, the incessant push-ups dished out to all of us for any minor infraction became much simpler when we realized that the sound of push-ups was just as good as an actual push-up. As you got into the push-up position between the bunks on the cold linoleum floor and began to push up and down, your metal dog tags would clank on the floor in a rhythmic fashion. However, as a drill sergeant walked up and down the aisles yelling at you and correcting your form, we soon learned that when his back was turned, you could simply clink your dog tags on the floor by hand in the same rhythm. This allowed you to take a break until he turned back around, at which point you would resume your push-ups as if you had never stopped exercising. It was small victories like this that made you feel you could survive.

I pushed it too far when I attempted to sneak a phone call home with another soldier from the sizable bank of payphones that encircled the covered courtyard. It was a stupid and ill-conceived plan that quickly got us both caught. Unfortunately, the temptation of hearing the voice of a loved one, even for a brief moment, was too overwhelming. The two of us were then brought before the drill sergeant, at which point we immediately confessed. A fitting resolution, consistent with the wisdom of King Solomon, was then handed down from behind the cheap wooden desk in the drill sergeant's office. The other telephonic criminal and I would walk in circles around the bank of payphones for two hours after lights out for a week. This would ensure that neither of us would do something so shortsighted and foolish in the future while also protecting the sparkling payphone sirens from any surreptitious visits from other homesick soldiers. Whether others were dissuaded by my late-night guard duty of Ma Bell's minions, I'll never know. But, with sleep being at such a premium, the loss of two hours each night for a week guaranteed that I would never make that particular mistake again.

Without a doubt, food was the biggest motivator throughout Basic Training. With so much physical exertion, food was always on my mind. I went to bed dreaming of breakfast and anxiously awaited lunch and dinner throughout the day's activities. There was no such thing as a snack or a midday candy bar. The ability to run to the kitchen for a handful of potato chips or a late-night bowl of cereal did not exist. Where an adult workplace may allow for an afternoon cup of coffee and a doughnut, Basic Training did not permit such civilized luxuries. As a result, you gobbled up everything you could eat whenever you could eat it. There was no room for pickiness. My body's constant clamoring for more calories turned taste buds into mere speed bumps as I shoveled any available food into my mouth. This ritual eventually backfired on one particular evening.

It was not uncommon for a drill sergeant to randomly pick out a few soldiers with a sweet and loving beckoning like, "Hey, you assholes, come with me." In just such a manner, I ended up on KP duty with several other recruits one evening. This meant that we had to clean up the kitchen, wash the dirty dishes that piled up during chow time, and take out the trash. Like a dazed and confused nomadic tribe wandering through the desert, this seemingly miserable assignment led us to an enticing mirage. What we saw, however, was not a figment of our imaginations. It was a freezer that housed innumerable frozen treats. The contents of the freezer seemed to glow as we first opened it to reveal dense piles of ice cream sandwiches, fudgesicles, creamsicles, and the fraternal twins of frigid temptation, the Good Humor Chocolate Éclair and Strawberry Shortcake bars. We took turns devouring package after package of prepackaged ice cream bars while the others kept watch. Being the ones throwing out the trash, the disposal of evidence was a piece of cake. The crime was perfect in its simplicity. Unfortunately, having been the recipient of an unrequested weekslong sugar detox program courtesy of the U.S. Army, my stomach was not ready for such a hasty onslaught of frozen fructose. After polishing off countless ice cream bars like hot dogs in a boardwalk hot dog eating contest, my stomach finally revolted, sending each bar back up in a technicolor milkshake display that I hastily deposited in the nearest latrine. If anyone ever tells you that you can never get too much of a good thing, don't believe them. I learned the patent absurdity of this claim while huddled over an Army toilet.

***

Basic Training went by with one day seamlessly blending into the next. Looking back on my time at Fort Benning, I am amazed at the creation of this large base and training center. As budding infantrymen, it was no great surprise that we walked everywhere. Running the risk of sounding like my parents and their reported childhood treks to school, the routes to and from the training ranges at Fort Benning were inarguably uphill both ways. I have no idea how they were able to accomplish such a feat. Like Stonehenge, it remains an unexplained miracle of architectural accomplishment.

Each day and each range site brought with it a new area of discovery and education. We were instructed in how to deploy and recover claymore antipersonnel mines and anti-tank mines. We were taught how to break down, clean, reassemble, and expertly shoot our M-16 rifles. They showed us how to use disposable shoulder-fired anti-tank weapons. On our hands and knees, we learned how to search a suspected minefield area with just a bayonet, a real-world situation I personally hoped to never encounter. We also spent multiple hours arming and properly throwing live and simulated hand grenades. This particular range was interesting, as we spent the morning throwing training grenades armed with blasting caps. We would pull the pin and throw the small metal orbs downrange at specified targets. Afterwards, we would recover the grenade bodies, return to our initial position, screw in a new blasting cap, and repeat the process. On one trip downrange to recover our grenade bodies, I retrieved a training grenade that had curiously lodged itself within the holes of a cinder block. Somehow, the spoon of the grenade had not dislodged when it was thrown. To my great surprise, the spoon flew off as I removed it from the cinder block, and the training grenade went off in my hand. The tiny explosions of the blasting caps were not strong enough to pierce the body of the metal grenades. Instead, the small resulting explosions were directed through the hole at the bottom of the grenade body. Unfortunately, that hole was directed at the palm of my right hand. Though no permanent damage was caused, the unanticipated burst shocked me and those in my general vicinity. It also left my hand stinging for several hours. Most importantly, it was a freak accident that reminded me of the enormity of what my fellow infantry hopefuls and I had gotten ourselves into. Given that the maximum effective range of a hand grenade was five meters, several of us would have been vaporized if this fluke mishap had occurred in the real world. It was a sobering thought.

It became increasingly apparent as we progressed through these days of training that everything we learned was designed either to kill others and break their equipment or to prevent ourselves from being killed. While some college students may begrudge the boring information they have to learn and regurgitate during their semesters at the local university, it became critically clear that our final examinations would be far more consequential if our services were ever called upon by the Commander in Chief. This stark realization certainly proved effective in keeping me engaged in our daily lessons. In the simplest of terms, what you didn't learn and master could kill you.

Like any course, some topics were more interesting than others. However, one particular range left me grappling with my own ideals of Christianity. The lesson of the day was bayonet fighting. My concerns began when I heard our drill sergeant repeatedly yell the following instructions...

"Simultaneously at the same time, withdraw your bayonet from your scavenger."

I felt a tinge of concern that this instructor did not realize that the words "simultaneously" and "at the same time" meant precisely the same thing. My concern grew beyond this grammatical faux pas when I realized that he was mistakenly referring to the "scabbards" that held our bayonets on our waists as a "scavenger." Still, the Army's ability to promote such butchers of the English language was not ultimately what caused my internal religious debate that day. As we affixed our bayonets to our rifles and began stabbing large canvas bags in pre-selected locations that were most likely to cause death, I began to wonder whether I could engage in such an act in the real world. Shooting someone from a distance of one hundred yards or more was one thing; plunging a knife into their body cavity while they were looking directly at you was another. My mind raced with questions of whether God condones such behavior. Would He forgive me if I had to do this to another human being? The internal debate grew louder as I watched some of my counterparts develop what appeared to be a bloodlust as they hooted and hollered after each plunge of the blade. On that day, the thought of killing someone in such a violent manner unsettled me. Many seemed to revel in this action. I did not. As a means of mental survival, I filed my thoughts and personal doubts into the dark recesses of my mind in a filing cabinet marked, "Things I Hope I Never Have to Do."

***

One thing that helped keep me grounded and allowed me to remain in touch with a sense of humanity was church. Given that church was such a significant part of our lives growing up, the ability to attend services on Sunday throughout Basic Training was a true blessing. For those wishing to go, a formation would be created, and we would be marched to the nearby chapel on Sunday mornings to attend services. I was always eager for this brief getaway. It offered an hour where you would not be screamed at or dropped for push-ups. But more importantly, it provided me an opportunity to reconnect with God. As I had called on His help repeatedly throughout the entire process of Basic

Training, it was nice to have a chance to thank Him for His assistance and to ask for His continued presence in my life.

One day, while walking down the main aisle of the chapel looking for an empty seat, I stumbled upon a neighbor from Norristown sitting in one of the pews. Unbeknownst to me, he also decided to join Uncle Sam's Army. We shook hands briefly and asked how each other was doing. He had arrived weeks after me and displayed the look of newness that I had undoubtedly shown myself not long ago. I wished him luck and took a seat. It was a chance encounter that reminded me of the people back home. It also made me realize that I was much closer to the finish line than he was. The thought made me feel happy for myself and sad for him all at once.

As I sat in the chapel, surrounded by others in camouflage uniforms, I looked at the beautiful stained-glass window depicting a soldier on his knee, leaning on his weapon and praying. I had stared at this colorful window each week. Though it was quite emotional, it also seemed inherently inconsistent. I had never been to a church in which an M-16 rifle was displayed. While I can now understand the intrinsic value and underlying message behind this moving image, all I could think at the time was, "Aw man. At Fort Benning, even God is in the Army."

***

Sadly, learning how to effectively and efficiently stab someone to death was not the worst day of training. That distinction belonged to the gas. I don't know if I'm alone in this feeling, but I have always been terrified of threats that you cannot see. It is one thing to see your enemy in front of you, but what about the enemy that has no face at all?

Given the very real possibility that enemies of the United States might use chemical weapons against U.S. troops and targets, we were trained in how to wear, deploy, and utilize gas masks. For days prior, our three drill sergeants joked about how it was coming. They laughed and encouraged us to eat a large breakfast that day so they could see everything we ate after we threw it up. They joked about how the gas couldn't wait to get us and how bad it was. In fact, one of the drill sergeants was so giddy with excitement that he kept singing lyrics from Michael Jackson's hit "Bad," which had been released two years earlier. Over and over, he repeated the following verse...

> Your butt is mine, gon' tell you right,
> Just show your face in broad daylight,

Then he would belt out the refrain: "Because I'm bad, I'm bad." He informed us that throughout the day, he and the other drill sergeants would be throwing canisters of CS gas at us to see how quickly we could remove our gas masks from the containers on our hips and put them on correctly to avoid the effects of the toxic agent. To spice up his torment, he noted that while we would never know when the gas was coming, we could expect to hear the first five notes of Michael Jackson's song: "Bom, Bom, Bom, Bom-Bom" before the canister was thrown. As the day progressed, while walking through the woods or gathered in a circle, we'd hear those dreaded five notes: "Bom, Bom, Bom, Bom-Bom."

Many times, no canister would be thrown into our area, and the drill sergeants would simply cackle in delight as their camouflaged baby chicks scrambled in sheer terror to get their gas masks on. Unfortunately, most of the time those five notes heralded the arrival of a smoking canister of CS gas thrown into the middle of our group as we went through the process over and over again. Theoretically, it was a great way to build muscle memory for a potentially life-saving action, but it was also a day of torment that frayed our nerves and kept us in a constant state of hypervigilance. All of that was bad enough, but the enjoyment that the drill sergeants seemed to be experiencing at our panic and torment really rubbed salt into the wounds.

CS gas is a commonly used tear gas employed by law enforcement worldwide for riot control, handling combative subjects, and resolving hostage situations. According to the National Library of Medicine, the microscopic particles of CS aerosol act as a "powdered barb" that attaches to moist skin and mucous membranes, causing irritation to the eyes, burning sensations, coughing, increased mucus secretion, severe headaches, dizziness, tightness in the chest, difficulty breathing, and excessive salivation for ten to thirty minutes. On this day, there were moments when you were quick enough to put your mask on properly to avoid the effects. However, sheer panic and the loss of fine motor control that accompanied it frequently made your attempts at self-protection ineffective. As the day wore on, we all experienced panicked minutes of burning and watering eyes, noses running in long, dripping sheets of mucus, stomach cramps, dry heaves, and sometimes not-so-dry heaves. As I bent over in my own private hell of burning, irritation, and vomiting, I watched one of my fellow recruits frantically claw at the dirt and bury his face in a hastily made hole like a dog, just to escape the seemingly unending wafts of CS gas.

To ensure that we each got a full taste of this delightful chemical agent, at the end of the day, they made us walk into a cinderblock room filled with CS gas. In small groups, we were ushered into the permeated room by our drill sergeants, who were protected by properly affixed gas masks. We were given the opportunity to don our gas masks prior to entering the room and we cautiously walked inside in small lines, holding onto the shoulder of the person in front of us. As we stood at attention in a small formation, we could barely see anything through the volume of CS gas swirling around the room. However, we could see how effective the masks were when they were properly placed on our heads. This marveling at the effectiveness of military equipment was short-lived, however, as we were ordered to remove our masks.

With no other choice, we counterintuitively took off the masks that were protecting us. To ensure that we got the full effect of the gas, they screamed at us to open our eyes. To confirm that we weren't holding our breath, we were instructed one by one to look at them, eyes open, and recite our respective Social Security numbers. As each of us completed our task, we were finally permitted to leave the building. This led to a mad dash for the exit. To this day, I have no idea which came first: was a tree planted directly outside the building, or was the building built directly in front of the tree? If the sadistic torture of the day was not enough, the location of a large oak directly outside the exit served as a parting blow of torment as one blinded, choking, and snot-covered soldier after another ran headfirst into the tree in their dash for fresh Georgia air. Some were able to avoid the mighty oak, while others collapsed on the ground upon impact with its unyielding girth. Though I was fortunate enough to have enough remaining vision to successfully juke the giant menace, one thing was becoming painfully apparent: maybe college would have been a better route.

***

These struggles and shared experiences of torture bonded us closer together as a platoon and as friends. Without realizing it, my early friend pool—largely marked by the boundaries of the Norristown borough limits—had now expanded to almost every state in the union. Jokes were shared, good-natured ribbing was routinely thrown around the barracks, and thanks to my own unique talents, imitations were made. Requests for imitations of Rocky Balboa, Arnold Schwarzenegger, and Clint Eastwood were often directed my way, and I was always more than happy to oblige. An imitation or two of a drill sergeant or fellow platoon mate also found their way into my repertoire. One imitation that was often met with laughter and references to my idiocy involved E.T. I accomplished this homage by putting gloves on my feet, squatting down, pulling my brown uniform t-shirt over my knees, and hanging my red-lensed flashlight on my dog tags so that it would shine through my shirt like E.T.'s glowing chest. I would then waddle through the barracks room, asking Elliot to phone home. I will be the first to admit, not all comedy is highbrow.

Another key time for socialization involved the nightly shining of our boots. Large groups of my fellow soldiers and I would often congregate in the stairwell landings to shine our boots together. This became a ritual of unit camaraderie as we talked about the day, exchanged wisecracks, and reminisced about home. Some conversations involved funny stories of friends and family, while others revolved around more painful personal situations. We learned which girlfriends couldn't stand the separation and decided that ending the relationship was in their best interest. This was always a traumatic event for the soldier who spent weeks clinging to the memory of their girl back home, using that memory as a beacon waiting for them at the end of their arduous journey. Sympathy was always readily available from the rest of the platoon in these situations. This ready sympathy likely stemmed from the fact that we all knew, deep down, we were one weekly phone call or 'Dear John' letter away from receiving the same heartbreaking news.

Other stories also surfaced as we shined our boots at night. One guy's father refused to take his calls home each week. Another guy's wife was forced to declare bankruptcy while he struggled through Basic Training. Yet another platoon mate learned that his best friend back home had shot himself. With no internet, cell phones, or FaceTime, this type of news was often received weeks later through payphone calls or mailed letters. Unlike today, news from home was not instantaneous. The claim that no news is good news was not true at that time. No news for us at Fort Benning in 1989 could also mean that the bad news simply hadn't reached us yet. This distinct possibility caused some hesitation in opening a letter from a girlfriend or calling home to parents.

Fortunately, the nightly shoe shine gatherings were not all doom and gloom. They were often marked by a requested sing-along with me as the band leader. As a fan of the oldies, I had taught others in the platoon Chuck Berry's classic "My Ding-A-Ling," which he released in 1972.

The song started with the lyrics:

> When I was a little bitty boy
> My grandmother bought me a cute little toy
> Silver bells hanging on a string
> She told me it was my ding-a-ling-a-ling.

While Chuck Berry's novelty song was ostensibly about the different venues where he played with this cute little toy and the difficulty he experienced in keeping both hands firmly placed on his ding-a-ling, only the densest among us would fail to realize that the toy was actually a euphemism for the most sensitive part of the artist's anatomy. Just like Chuck Berry did in the live version of his song, I separated the platoon into two groups for the refrain. Together, the groups would skillfully belt out, "My ding-a-ling, my ding-a-ling, I want you to play with my ding-a-ling." Then everyone would laugh, and we would continue with the subsequent verses. The crescendo of laughter would always reach its tipping point when I used the final verse of the song to accuse those in the platoon who were not singing with us of playing with their own ding-a-ling.

As rap was becoming increasingly popular in the late eighties, I was routinely requested to string rhyming verses together, accompanied by a beat provided by my platoon mates banging on the ammunition cans that held their boot-shining supplies. These raps poked fun at the unique quirks of those in the platoon. Prior to each shoe shine, I had to come up with a new verse to tease the next person in line. While I don't recall all of these verses, I remember good-naturedly mocking the first alphabetical person in our platoon—his last name was Alexander. The poor guy was so tense and focused on passing Basic Training that he would talk in his sleep at night. He was often heard yelling, "I have to meet the standards. I have to meet the standards." This led to my masterful lyric: "Let me tell you 'bout my main man Alexander. All he really cares about is meeting those standards." People would crack up and clap as I slowly made my way down the bunks, teasing the next guy in line.

While some may find it unkind to tease those around you, this is actually how guys develop a sense of belonging. I found this to be true on the various sports teams I played for growing up, and the Army proved no different. In fact, when it comes to male bonding, you are probably not incredibly well thought of if you do not have a nickname or were not teased at some point. In Basic Training at Fort Benning, we were all identified by a number within the platoon; I was number 113. As the weeks went by and the ribbing continued, we began to refer to each other by last names, and eventually nicknames. With those you became closest to, you might actually come to call them by their first names. This was a sign of the truest and closest friendships.

***

The ability to start goofing around more freely was made possible once we moved from Basic Training to Advanced Individual Training. AIT, as the Army calls it, is akin to attending a trade school. For many specialties within the Army, new soldiers start their journey with Basic Training at one facility to learn the basic skills of soldiering, only to be transferred to a different facility to learn their new specialized skill set. Since all my fellow soldiers and I had chosen the career path of an infantryman, we stayed at Fort Benning for our AIT. While all new soldiers learn the basics of how to kill enemy soldiers and disable their equipment, infantry AIT involved a more in-depth exploration of these skills. As such, the transition between Basic Training and AIT was not immediately discernible. In fact, we had to be informed by the drill sergeants that we were beginning this new phase of our training. This phase introduced lessons in more advanced weapons and tactics. Of particular note was the day we waited our turn at a dirt track while a tank made incessant circles around the loop. When it was finally our turn, we ran onto the track, dove into a shallow hole, and then waited for the tank to drive over our position. Once the tank passed, we were instructed to jump up from our place of concealment and use an inert shoulder-fired antitank weapon to simulate shooting at the rear of the tank.

We also practiced land navigation, traversing the woods with a map, a compass, and knowledge of our pace count (the number of left steps that made up 100 meters). As budding infantrymen, we marched everywhere carrying loads of equipment, the longest of which was a planned 20-mile road march. This trek tested our endurance and demonstrated to each of us that we were more capable and resilient than we ever realized. To highlight this point even further, we participated in a nighttime live-fire exercise. En masse, we were instructed to crawl on our stomachs through mud and under barbed wire while explosions and smoke grenades detonated around us. The most crucial instruction of that evening was to keep our heads down and, under absolutely no circumstances, to stand up. The reason for this instruction was clear: M-60 machine guns were being fired downrange over our heads throughout the exercise. Simply put, standing up guaranteed immediate death.

The purpose of this exercise was painfully clear: war is hell. By exposing us to the sounds of explosions, the disorientation of darkness illuminated by flares, the putrid smell of smoke grenades, and the sight and sound of 7.62mm glowing tracer rounds being fired overhead, we would hopefully become somewhat desensitized to the real thing if and when it happened. So, we crawled on our bellies for what seemed like a mile until we finally reached a point of safety, relieved to know that we had not become the subject of one of the stories you occasionally hear about training fatalities.

Not only did AIT bring these new experiences, but it also introduced a palpable sense of relaxation. Little rewards began to materialize: trips to the PX to buy junk food were now permitted, we had the opportunity to see a movie, and we were finally allowed to listen to a Walkman in the evenings. Perhaps most monumental of all was the ability to stay up until 9:30 p.m. and sleep until 6:00 a.m. All of these changes gradually made us feel more human. Even the drill sergeants became more relaxed. Slowly, the incessant yelling was replaced with occasional joking. I can recall one occasion when I was joking around with one of the drill sergeants, and he placed his Smokey the Bear hat on my head. This action would have been unthinkable weeks earlier and felt like a strange mixture of Mean Joe Greene throwing his game jersey to a young kid in the classic Coke commercial and the Pope placing his hat on your head. Everyone, especially me, was awestruck by this simple act. Unsure what to do, I began imitating the yelling and berating behavior of the earlier version of our drill sergeant. The stunned silence among the group was soon replaced by laughter at my imitation. Even more surprising was the fact that the drill sergeant joined in on the laughter. He then snatched his hat from my head and said, "Give me that back, you asshole." This exchange answered a question that had rattled around in my head for months: I guess the drill sergeants actually were human.

***

Unlike the soldiers, marines, airmen, and sailors of today's military, the enemy we were training against in 1989 was not terrorists. We were training to fight the Soviet Union. This point was driven home one day when we were ushered into a room and seated in a circle. It was explained that we had a guest who had been brought in to speak with us. A mix of fanfare and secrecy set the stage for this guest. We were informed that the person who was about to enter the room was a defector from the Soviet Union and that we were to treat him with respect as he told his story. A man was then quietly escorted to the center of our circle. He walked around the middle of our group and talked about his life in the Soviet Union and why he had defected to the United States. Although fascinating, things took an ugly turn when he inexplicably began to discuss the strength of the Soviet Union and the inherent weakness of the United States. Grumblings and anger spread among our platoon as we listened to this man's point of view. The situation became much more personal when he began to pontificate on how tough Soviet soldiers were and how unprepared the U.S. Army and the other branches of the American military were for a toe-to-toe battle with the Soviet military. Any such encounter, he assured us, would lead to a crushing defeat for the United States. This was the straw that broke the camel's back. The grumblings escalated into an all-out verbal assault on this piece of human refuse that had been brought into our midst. I became particularly vocal in this one-sided debate and screamed at him, asking if his country was so great, why did he leave it to come to the United States? Others joined in, promising that we would destroy the Soviet Army while he vehemently disagreed. My threats and those of my platoon mates continued to escalate until the disgusting Soviet visitor was finally and quickly hurried from the room as we cheered his cowardly departure.

I have always felt that this whole event was nothing more than a charade designed to harness our hatred of an enemy we had never actually met. Even at that time, as an 18-year-old kid, I suspected the event was a setup. Despite my suspicions, I personally fell for the bait hook, line, and sinker. My love for the United States and my determination to defend its people from all enemies, foreign and domestic, especially from the godless heathens of the Soviet Union, had reached its zenith. Again, the United States Army was many things, but it was not stupid. They succeeded in tearing me down and then building me back up as a soldier. They succeeded in teaching me how to kill the enemy. They succeeded in fostering a deep commitment to my fellow platoon mates. They succeeded in stoking the fires of my patriotism, and now they had successfully fostered a deep hatred of our communist enemies. Their plan was both sneaky and ingenious. The only remaining question was where I would serve our great nation.

***

For many, myself included, receiving orders about our stationing after AIT was a source of stress. My primary concern was getting home for Christmas. Once it was finally revealed that we would, in fact, be permitted to take leave for Christmas between graduating and reporting to our first duty station, a huge weight was lifted from my shoulders. In truth, my first duty station was not as great a concern at that moment. This sense of calm stemmed from the assurance I had received from my recruiter back in Norristown that, since my enlistment was only for two years, I would most likely stay at Fort Benning. So, as we reported to the formation area to receive our orders, I felt more excitement about hearing where my friends would be stationed than I was worried about my own news. Then, a small number of us were called to the front of the formation. I was pleasantly surprised to learn how many of my friends would be staying with me in Georgia.

The drill sergeant then looked at our small group and informed us that we were being assigned to Germany. I can assure you, in no uncertain terms, that having the unenviable honor of being the first person in the history of the United States Army to be lied to by his recruiter is not a distinction I am glad to hold. But there it was. Everything seemed to move in slow motion from that point forward as I processed what I had just learned. Perhaps they mistook me for another soldier? After all, we all had shaved heads and dressed in identical uniforms. Surely a mistake was possible. Better yet, both "Georgia" and "Germany" start with the same two letters. Perhaps the drill sergeant misread the orders. Now that was a distinct possibility. Let's not forget that one of the drill sergeants thought our bayonets were kept in a "scavenger" instead of a "scabbard." I'm sure they just misread "Georgia." I think in God's infinite wisdom, the crushing blow of reality can sometimes act like a smelling salt, and I was jolted back into coherence. I moved aside so that the next group could be informed of their orders. Confusion, disorientation, and trepidation engulfed me as I processed the news.

As we reunited as a platoon, discussions bounced around the walls of the barracks room. Some were happy; many were not. But ultimately, like most things in the Army, all you could do was sit there and take it. What choice did you have? "Hey, Sarge? Germany isn't going to work for me. What else do you have?"

"I'd like to quit now, please."

"I'd like to speak to a manager."

None of these approaches were going to work. So instead, you complained to your platoon mates, you whined to your parents, and you quietly shed a tear or two on your pillow after lights out. One thing was for certain, however: those four years of German I took in high school were going to come in handy... because I was going to Germany. God help me. Or should I say, "Gott hilf mir."

4

GRADUATION

The mood was electric. All of the hard work and torture was complete. We had finally become Infantrymen. In Army jargon, we were now considered "Eleven Bravos", a reflection of the 11B Military Occupational Specialty (MOS) designation for infantry personnel. Per the Army's own verbiage, we were now qualified to serve in the field, to defend the United States against any ground threat, to capture, destroy, and deter enemy forces, to assist in reconnaissance, and to help mobilize troops and weaponry to support the mission as the ground combat force. For me, this was a huge accomplishment and a great source of pride. Not only was I now a legitimate member of the United States Army, but I had not taken the easy route. I was not a cook, a supply technician, or a payroll specialist; I was an Infantryman. Along with my fellow platoon mates, we had survived the Army's Infantry School. Starting it was terrifying, and going through it was grueling. But on this side of the ordeal, I felt nothing but pride and accomplishment. Regardless of where our lives and military careers took us, no one would ever be able to take that 11B designation away from us.

At Fort Benning, becoming a full-fledged member of the United States Army Infantry was marked by the "Turning

Blue" ceremony. This small ceremony occurs the day before graduation and receives its name from the two key indicators of an Infantryman's uniform. The first is the infantry cord, which is light blue—more appropriately identified as "infantry blue"—and made up of a series of interlocking square knots around a center cord. One at a time, the company commander walked down the line and affixed the infantry cord under our right arm and around the shoulder of our Class A uniforms. Along with the infantry blue discs worn under the gold branch and U.S. insignias on our lapels, we were now immediately identifiable as members of the United States Army Infantry. For all of the infantrymen who came before us and those who would come after us, it was a distinction that was well-earned and not easily attained. We were all now part of a brotherhood.

As it was December, graduation the following day was cold but sunny. My parents had driven down from Norristown, and their pride was palpable. As platoons, we marched into graduation in perfect unison, heralded by the marching band. We entered this grand training process as varied individuals from different states across the country. The transformation was undeniable to those in attendance as we looked and maneuvered as one. Our country's motto of "e pluribus unum" was alive and well that day, demonstrating the ability of the personnel assigned to the Infantry School at Fort Benning to effectively and efficiently create one cohesive unit from many assorted and unrelated individuals.

The ceremony featured congratulatory speeches, poignant selections played by the Army band, crisp salutes, and, of course, a recitation of the Star-Spangled Banner. It seemed as if the whispers of all of America's soldiers, from the Battle of Saratoga in the Revolutionary War to the Battle of Hamburger Hill in Vietnam, were carried in on the crisp December breeze. The joy we all experienced at finally finishing our training was matched in scope by the realization that we stood on the shoulders of those who came before us to protect our great nation. We were next in line should the alarm sound. It was a humbling realization.

As the pomp and circumstance came to a close, we were finally permitted to do the one thing that all of us had dreamed of for the last three and a half months: to see our families. The crowds of soldiers and civilians melded into one as loved ones reunited. I hugged my parents tightly as I watched others do the same. Tears were abundant during this long-awaited reunion of family members and their freshly minted soldiers. Platoon families introduced one another to their birth families, finally affording them the opportunity to put faces to the names they had heard so much about in letters, hurried phone calls, and barracks conversations. We showed our parents and families around our home of the last 14 weeks, allowing them to contextualize our tales. And then it was done. Where we had entered Fort Benning as a tattered group of frightened faces and panicked movements, we left with smiles and heartfelt hugs. Over the last few days, many of us made it a point to collect personal information from one another as a means of staying in touch. In 1989, with no internet, email, cell phones, or social media, there was no way to reconnect. While there would be some calls to the civilian homes of my platoon mates over the upcoming Christmas holiday season, once everyone scattered to their next duty stations, future contact became difficult. Unlike today, there was no ability to call a friend on his cellphone or message him on Snapchat. As a result, the majority of those important and meaningful relationships simply faded away. It is strange to consider how people who had been such a huge part of your life under grueling conditions can just disappear. Upon graduation, we were all so excited to leave with our families that the farewells felt insufficient and incomplete. Although the goodbyes were casual, for many of us, they were also final.

As I threw my duffle bag stuffed with government-issued clothing into the trunk of my dad's car and settled into the backseat for the long drive home, something unexpected happened. I began to cry. They were not just tears; they were sobs. They were not tears of happiness but of sadness. This caused me obvious confusion. Like many in the platoon, I had immediately regretted my decision to join the Army when I first arrived at Fort Benning. Basic Training and AIT were periods of profound homesickness and heartache for many of us. Each day was marked by an unrelenting desire to leave and return home. Every day was simply a countdown until the misery was over. Now, as I prepared for the long-awaited return home, I found myself saddened by the loss of my 49 new family members to whom I had no blood relation. In one fell swoop, the people with whom I had spent so much time eating, sleeping, training, sweating, and laughing just disappeared. It was at that moment in my life that I realized that "home" is not a specific dot on a map but a place where the ones you care about most are located. In that sense, "home" is a relative term, and I was as shocked as anyone that I was shedding a tear over leaving one home to return to another.

Luckily, my sadness was short-lived. It was quickly replaced by unbridled joy as my parents and I stopped for lunch. I have no memory of where we ate, but I will never forget the vigor with which I approached the meal. I ate as if I had just returned to civilization after a prolonged absence on a desert island. The habit of consuming as much food as quickly as possible lingered with me for days after graduation. With no drill sergeants to impose artificial limits on my intake, I still reflexively swallowed giant gulps of food in hasty forkfuls. Without a ticking clock dictating how long I could speak with my parents, I talked and talked and talked. There was so much I needed to get off my chest—so many stories to share.

As we returned to the car, I found one more Maslow-like need waiting for me: sleep. Lying down in the back seat, I closed my eyes... just for a minute. In reality, I slept for hour after hour. With no drill sergeant lurking about, I dozed off as my poor father made the long drive home without stopping. Unfortunately, he was forced to navigate through a snowstorm that seemed to envelop the entire eastern seaboard. But so determined was he to get me home that he never stopped... and I never woke up. I suppose one thing the Army did not teach me was the common courtesy of sharing drive time on a long car trip.

***

Christmas was always a wonderful event in our house, and my mom went to painstaking lengths each year decorating, shopping, wrapping gifts, baking, and cooking. As with everything else in my life, the joy of that particular Christmas season felt magnified because it seemed earned through the months of training at Fort Benning and the repeated threats to me and my fellow soldiers that we would miss Christmas this year. It was great to see extended family at Christmas Eve dinner, and I felt a tremendous amount of pride wearing my Class A uniform that evening, especially the infantry blue cord around my right shoulder. As expected, everyone in church fussed over my uniform and my return to Norristown. Sadly, in the back of my mind, the clock was always ticking. Despite the fun and festivities, January was approaching, and I would soon be heading off for a new adventure that I neither chose nor looked forward to.

5

GERMANY

The time to leave again had come quickly, whether I wanted it to or not. As a child, I had always hated when the Christmas break ended and we had to return to school. The end of the holiday season and all the fun and festivities made the night before the first day back at school a sleepless one. But now, I would not be returning to school as in years past. Instead, I would be departing the country to start a new leg of my military service. All the unknowns associated with this new journey multiplied the annual sadness brought about by the end of the Christmas season exponentially.

It had snowed incessantly on the day of my departure, and my poor father once again had to drive through driving snow because of my commitment to the United States Army. But unlike the ride from Fort Benning, this drive was not to bring me home but to send me even farther away. Although the flight was supposed to leave in the afternoon, the bad weather led to delay after delay. Where many people often note the value of ripping things off like a band-aid—especially goodbyes—this day proved to be the exact opposite. I would get close to departure time and the obvious emotional wave that accompanied it, only to learn that the flight was delayed. My parents and I battled between the joy of having another hour or so together and the discouragement brought on by yet another delay of the inevitable. And so it went for hour after hour.

At long last, in the early morning hours of the following day, I finally boarded the jetway and turned to see both of my parents crying. It is one thing to hurt yourself; it is another to see the hurt you are causing someone else. With a sad wave, I then boarded the plane that would take me to Europe. God works in mysterious ways. Whether I was willing to see it or not, I was actually glad to finally be leaving. The emotional roller coaster caused by the incessant delays throughout the day was reaching an unbearable level. Finally boarding the plane brought with it a sense of relief that seemed to counterbalance the sadness. I was grateful for anything that helped ease my departure.

Upon arriving in Frankfurt, I was gathered with various other soldiers who had made their way to Germany but had not yet received specific orders as to where they would be assigned. We were housed together and awaited word of our final destinations. Somewhere along the line, we received information that two options were available: we would either be assigned to an installation near a small town in West Germany or to Berlin. For reasons still unknown to me, I secretly hoped I would be tapped for Berlin. Perhaps my desire stemmed from the fact that I had at least heard of Berlin; it also may have been that Berlin simply sounded cooler. Whatever the reason, my secret wish came true, and I was soon placed on a train bound for Berlin.

✹✹✹

At the time of my arrival, Berlin was a very unique place. After the defeat of Nazi Germany in World War II, the four victorious allies—the United States, England, France, and the Soviet Union—established occupation zones in Germany. The Soviet Union's occupation zone was in the east, while the U.S., England, and France established their zones in the west. While Berlin was located deep within the Soviet Union's occupational zone, the city itself was given special status. Like a miniature version of Germany, Berlin was divided in half, with the Soviet Union taking the eastern part of the city while the U.S., England, and France split the western part into three distinct zones. This separation caused Berlin to become known as "the divided city." As the Cold War ushered in a stark military and ideological divide between the Soviet Union and the West, two distinct German states were founded in 1949: the Federal Republic of Germany (West Germany) and the German Democratic Republic (East Germany). As the former capital of Germany during World War II, Berlin became the heart of the Cold War, with the eastern half of the city blanketed by governmental oppression of its citizens and the western half promising a gateway to freedom and opportunity. It was the line of scrimmage as the East faced off against the West.

The East German people were in such close proximity to the liberty offered in West Germany that they could see with their own eyes the tangible benefits of living in a free society. The stark difference in lifestyles soon created a large wave of migration from East Germany to West Germany. This mass exodus stood as an unmistakable repudiation of Soviet ideology. In response, construction of the Berlin Wall began in August 1961to stem the tide of those seeking to escape the oppression of East Germany. What started as rolls of barbed wire guarded by East German officials quickly morphed into concrete walls 15 feet high, topped with barbed wire and protected by watchtowers, attack dogs, and landmines. While the Soviet Union's "Iron Curtain" was a figurative philosophical and political border separating its communist empire from the freedoms of the West, the 27-mile-long Berlin Wall served as a physical reminder of this separation. My new assignment, the Berlin Brigade, was a brigade-sized unit positioned on the western side of the Berlin Wall to deter Soviet aggression and defend the city of Berlin from the Soviet Union should it ever attempt to expand into West Germany.

I had the opportunity to observe firsthand the unmistakable differences between East and West when my unit had to travel through East Berlin. This required us to cross through the Berlin Wall at the famous access point known as Checkpoint Charlie. As we entered East Berlin, it seemed as if the skies immediately darkened. I'm certain there is no meteorological explanation for why the sunny blue skies of West Germany would have turned overcast on the opposite side of the Berlin Wall, but I am convinced they did. The buildings, the clothing, and even the complexions of the East German people also seemed to turn gray after passing through the wall. We were given the opportunity to use the restrooms in East Berlin, and I sprinted out of the bathroom stall with a handful of toilet paper. I had to show the rest of my unit the sandpaper-like texture of communist toilet tissue. While I could have sanded a table leg with it, I am not sure I would want to apply it to my cushy American derriere. Communist oppression seemed to come in all forms. No wonder the East German residents seemed so unhappy.

***

Upon my initial arrival in Berlin, I was assigned to Charlie Company, 4th Battalion, 502d Infantry Regiment. As highlighted in the introductory information I was provided, this battalion, also referred to as the "Swift Strike Battalion," was born to fight. It was activated on March 2, 1942, as Delta Company, 502d Parachute Infantry Regiment, and was deployed overseas as part of the 101st Airborne Division. On June 6, 1944, soldiers of the 502d Parachute Infantry Regiment parachuted into the darkness to seize key objectives that were critical to the success of the landing on D-Day. The unit went on to fight in other bloody battles with the Nazis during the invasion of Holland and while defending Bastogne during the Battle of the Bulge. Twenty years later, units of the 502d continued their fighting tradition in 15 major campaigns during the Vietnam War. As it was explained to new arrivals in 1989:

"Today, as in years past, the 4th Battalion of the 502d Infantry stands ready to fight at a moment's notice. We are face-to-face with a powerful enemy that threatens the free world and the city of West Berlin. The soldiers of this battalion are as ready and determined as the soldiers of the Regiment's past."

The mission of the 4th Battalion of the 502d Infantry Regiment of the Berlin Brigade was clearly and unequivocally explained as follows:

"We serve in Berlin as an unmistakable demonstration of United States and Allied resolve to keep West Berlin free. Stand tall as Americans in the defense of freedom. Set an example that America can be proud of. We are an infantry battalion and must be prepared to fight and win. Focus on combat missions. Prepare for war today."

There was no doubt about our proximity to Soviet forces, and we were constantly reminded of the need for operational security. It was immediately explained to each of us arriving at the Berlin Brigade that Subversion and Espionage Directed Against the U.S. Army (referred to as "SAEDA") was a real threat in Berlin. It was made abundantly clear: "The enemy is here, among us, looking for a weakness. If you are approached, report it immediately. Keep our plans and readiness status safe from the enemy." Essentially, this was our updated version of the World War II adage, "Loose Lips Sink Ships."

Unlike other military installations scattered across the globe, we were a stone's throw away from the second most powerful military in the world, which understandably impacted the way we lived. Whereas other units simply threw on their camouflaged battle dress uniforms (BDUs), ours had to be ironed and creased. Our boots had to be shined. We knew that the Soviets were watching us at all times, and it was believed that an observable crispness in our appearance reflected organization, professionalism, and strength as a unit. So close were our enemies that we were constantly reminded to be on the lookout for small black sedans driving in and around the city. These vehicles were believed to be carrying intelligence officers from the KGB. We were also given specific instructions when using area payphones to call home to our families. More specifically, we were informed that once we picked up the telephone, we were to say "Hello Boris" into the handset. Given the very real possibility that the Soviets may have tapped these lines of communication, this instruction served as a reminder for us to be mindful of what we said over the telephone. Similarly, it notified any Soviets who might actually be listening in that we were practicing good operational security and they would be wasting their time listening to our conversations any further. Despite this healthy fear of our Soviet counterparts on the other side of the wall, something of profound and world-altering importance occurred a handful of weeks before my arrival in Germany. The Berlin Wall, perhaps the greatest symbol of the Cold War, had begun to fall.

***

In 1985, the Soviet Politburo elected Mikhail Gorbachev as General Secretary. As the new Soviet leader, Gorbachev introduced two key reform policies: "Glasnost" (Openness) and "Perestroika" (Restructuring). However, these two policies could barely keep up with the revolutionary movements simmering in several Eastern Bloc countries. In the following years, countries like Poland, Bulgaria, Estonia, Latvia, Lithuania, Hungary, and Czechoslovakia began to demonstrate a desire for independence from their Soviet oppressors. Free elections, demonstrations, revolutions of varying degrees, and the opening of borders that permitted the escape of East Germans yearning to breathe free all marked the buckling of the once impermeable Iron Curtain. Then, in October 1989, seventy thousand demonstrators in the East German city of Leipzig took to the streets demanding democracy. Other East German cities soon followed suit. By November, approximately half a million demonstrators had gathered in East Berlin. After a poorly delivered bureaucratic message suggested that travel restrictions would be loosened for East Germans seeking to travel to West Germany, thousands of demonstrators flocked to Brandenburg Gate in Berlin and began chipping away at the cement wall with hammers and pickaxes. Thus began the fall of the Berlin Wall and, eventually, the Soviet Union.

During my visits to the wall, I saw giant holes in the once mighty barrier. Looking through the wall were East German and Soviet troops. Growing up during the Cold War and being fed a steady diet of anti-communist rhetoric, I was fascinated to see the enemy looking directly back at me. It was not lost on me that it was the oppression of the East that was gazing through a gaping hole toward the freedom of the West, and not the other way around. Although these young soldiers looked like me, the separation went far beyond the design of their uniforms and the side of the border from which they observed. This was the enemy. This was who would be shooting at me and vice versa if situations and circumstances were different. But at that moment, it felt like being at a zoo, where you could stare from a safe distance at a creature that was clearly capable of killing you. It was a telling moment in my life and a previously unthinkable wrinkle in the complicated history of not only Germany but the world as a whole.

***

When I first arrived at my new platoon area, I began to meet some of my new coworkers as I was shown around our barracks. I was definitely the low man on the totem pole, as many of these soldiers had already been in the unit for years. This realization really hit home when I was introduced to a member of my new platoon who seemed extremely relaxed as he chilled in his barracks room. There are two key things I remember from this exchange. The first was that he had a giant blue flag emblazoned with a large yellow "M." Having lived my entire life in the greater Philadelphia area, I was not immediately aware of what this flag represented until this new acquaintance informed me that he was from Michigan. Though I didn't know it at the time, this flag from the University of Michigan would ultimately become a much more significant part of my future life. The second memorable part of this introduction was that the young man before me had only two weeks left before he separated from the Army. He was quite happy and excited about this fact, and I felt quite jealous. With 24 months to go, I could only imagine what it must feel like to be so close to finishing your military commitment.

As I was shown around the floor where on-base residents of my new platoon lived and introductions continued, my guide told everyone I met that I would be sharing a room with Solomon (I have changed this name to protect the guilty).

The revelation that I would be rooming with a guy named Solomon was routinely met with guffaws and condolences.

"Hopefully you can square that guy away," was the gist of most of the comments.

Quickly, I was learning that Solomon was a problem child. Of course, I would end up with the problem child. I was brand new to both the Berlin Brigade and the country of Germany, and I was battling my own homesickness. I had not yet collected myself. How was I going to square away another troop who had been here longer than me?

When I was finally shown my room, I was glad to see that it was far different from the accommodations of Basic Training. The room was a large square separated into three living areas by six wall lockers. To the left and right rear were small rooms approximately 10'x10'. Immediately upon entering, there was a larger area about 10'x20'. I was greeted by a soldier from the left rear area who smiled and shook my hand. Although he looked distinctly different from me, there was nothing about him that screamed "Problem Child." The affable young man had dark skin and jet-black stubble where a civilian head of hair would have been. He introduced himself as "Chuck," and I noticed a slight accent that I was not familiar with. As we exchanged pleasantries, I learned that Chuck was a full-blooded Navajo Indian from New Mexico. He cautioned me about our third roommate, Solomon. No wonder Chuck did not seem to be a problem; he was not the one I had been warned about.

Chuck turned out to be a good guy and a good roommate. His background was extremely interesting to me, and he often shared stories about his life growing up in the Navajo tribe. We talked about American Indian folklore and what life was like on the reservation. Instead of writing letters, Chuck's family would send him cassette tapes of audio well-wishes. I would often hear him listening to the tapes out loud and laughing at a foreign and indecipherable language that informed him of things back home. It was not uncommon for him to yell over the wall lockers to me, "Did you understand that, Beyer?" Being non-fluent in Navajo, I would sarcastically reply with things like, "Oh yeah, Chuck. That was funny." He would then offer me a quick translation of what his family was telling him, and we would both laugh. Through these interactions, I came to realize that everyone has different backgrounds, lifestyles, and experiences. I also learned that most people take great pride in where they come from, whether it be a state, a city, a neighborhood, or, in Chuck's case, a tribe. This made communicating with the people I met in the Army very easy because everyone had a story to tell.

Chuck's biggest weakness, however, was his drinking. The man could drink beer as easily as the rest of us could drink water from a canteen. From what I could tell, beer had no physiological effect on him. Unfortunately, with every superpower comes a vulnerability. For Chuck, his kryptonite was liquor. It seemed that even a drop of liquor entering his system transformed the happy-go-lucky Chuck into an enraged pugilist. It was like watching Bill Bixby morph into Lou Ferrigno in the old "Incredible Hulk" television show. However, it was not rage that brought this Mr. Jekyll to life; it was the hard stuff. Luckily, his rage was never directed at me. As a result, there were many occasions when I helped Chuck into bed to sleep it off after he sought out arenas where he could try to take his shot at the title with one of our fellow soldiers. Just like Basic Training, I realized that the world was made up of all kinds of people. But every once in a great while, you come across a true character. For me and Chuck, as well as for the rest of our platoon, that character was Solomon.

Shortly after Chuck and I made our introductions, our other roommate, Solomon, entered the room. He was tall and had an inherently goofy look about him. It did not take long to see what the others were talking about. The elevator simply did not reach the top floor for this young soldier. He had his own unique way of speaking, but it was not a discernible accent like Chuck's. Instead, he had a nasally voice, a profound lisp, and a hint of baby talk. This combination made him appear cognitively impaired. Whether he actually was cognitively impaired was a call best left to the professionals. One thing was for certain, however: he was the poster child for what can happen when U.S. Army recruiters are forced to meet their quarterly recruitment quotas.

I learned that Solomon was from Pensacola, Florida, which he pronounced as "Pentha-Col-Wa, Fwo-wida." As time went by, the platoon and I realized the depths of Solomon's intellectual deficits. I remember one occasion when Chuck, Solomon, and I were discussing our homes. When it became apparent that Solomon did not have a working knowledge of Florida geography, Chuck asked if Solomon knew what city was the capital of Florida. Solomon responded with an unwarranted degree of confidence, "Tennessee." This obviously evoked laughter from both Chuck and me. When I informed him that the capital was actually Tallahassee, he furrowed his brow in confusion and corrected me, saying, "No, I'm pwetty sure it's Tenna-She."

On another occasion, Chuck and I could hear Solomon on his side of the room becoming increasingly irritated. This was not typically a tough code to crack, as his frustration tended to manifest in a loud, lispy noise that sounded much like an old steam locomotive starting to move. After Solomon's fifth or sixth "shush," both Chuck and I peeked around our wall lockers to see what was causing Solomon so much frustration.

"What's wrong now?" I asked.

With a furrowed brow and a discernible look of confusion, Solomon began his explanation as he gazed down at a handful of military documents. He was frustrated by the fact that while he had supposedly enlisted in the Army for four years, his orders noted that he had enlisted for three years, eleven months, and thirty days. This didn't make sense to him.

I clarified that three years, eleven months, and thirty days amounted to four total years. My clarification not only confused him but also served to increase his irritability. As such, I decided to take him back to the basics with a simple question.

"How many days are there in a month?" I asked.

"Thwee hundwed and thixty-five," he answered.

Astonished by this level of ignorance, I held onto the hope that maybe he thought I asked how many days were in a year. "No," I continued, "How many days are in a month?"

"Oh," he pondered before answering, "Thix hundwed and thirty-five."

Chuck exploded into laughter. "Jesus, Solomon, there are thirty days in a month," Chuck yelled between laughs.

Solomon's brow furrowed even deeper as he yelled back, "Now you guys got me all confuthed."

It amazed me that he had passed any type of military aptitude testing. It could be argued that every person has strengths and weaknesses. Unfortunately for Solomon, he appeared to possess only a series of gradually increasing weaknesses. In addition to being the last in line for handouts from the brain factory, he was also physically weak, incredibly lazy, exhibited atrocious decision-making, and seemed averse to any sort of basic hygiene. This meant that his part of the room always looked as if someone had left the window open and a strong breeze had played havoc with his personal belongings. Even more problematic was the fact that his portion of the room also emanated an unpleasant odor, reminiscent of smoke rising from a campfire. This proved to be an issue for Chuck and me, as Solomon's area was the only visible portion of the room when anyone opened the door. Because the Army values organization and order, Solomon's lack of tidiness meant frequent push-ups for all three of us, even though Chuck and I kept our parts of the room clean and tidy. I can only assume that the reason for this mass punishment of all the room's occupants by our Squad Leader and Platoon Sergeant was to encourage Chuck and me to motivate Solomon, where others had failed to do so. As such, I took the cleaning skills of my obsessive-compulsive mother and tried to pass them on to Solomon. I showed him how to Pledge his desk, organize his belongings, vacuum his area of the room, and even how to align his shoes under his bunk. This last task was particularly nauseating, as it required me to touch his running shoes, which not only smelled otherworldly but also had holes above the big toe where his long toenails had gradually torn through the fabric. At no time did I read about any of this responsibility in the infantry promotional materials.

My efforts to teach him to clean would last only a day or two before the true Solomon returned. In many ways, it was like trying to teach a preschooler quantum physics; he simply could not grasp the concepts I was trying to explain to him. However, everyone has a breaking point. My patience with Solomon came to an abrupt end over his personal hygiene. I can recall one particular instance in which his bodily funk wafted over my wall lockers and seemed to hover over my bunk like a low-lying English fog. Unable to sleep from the nauseating aroma, I grabbed a can of Glade air freshener and sprayed the fragrant aerosol over his body and sheets as he slept. Although he did not awaken from my actions, I soon did. Despite a brief respite from his stench, the new cloud hovering just above me now smelled like a fragrant mixture of Glade and ass. It appeared that in my haste, I had unwittingly created a previously undiscovered scent called "GLASS." I can assure you, under no circumstances will you be seeing this fragrance on your store shelves anytime soon.

***

Solomon's lack of hygiene and laziness combined for another memorable moment. Because he also lacked athleticism, Solomon routinely drew attention to himself during physical training (PT), leading to him constantly being dropped for push-ups. After our Squad Leader finished punishing Solomon with push-ups one Friday morning, he ordered Solomon to get a haircut by formation on Monday morning, as his hair was becoming unruly. Solomon responded simply, "Yeth, Thergeant."

This should have been a task that Solomon had no problem accomplishing. After all, not only was he given a direct order, but he had several days and various barber shops available to him. In light of the uncharacteristic anger displayed by our Squad Leader that particular morning, the guy in the room next to ours must have felt bad for Solomon because he offered to cut Solomon's hair for him with his personal set of hair clippers. And so it began.

Throughout the weekend, our neighbor repeatedly asked if Solomon was ready for him to cut his hair. Solomon continued to brush him off, opting instead to sit in his own filth while playing video games and watching television. For me, it was like watching a slow-motion train wreck. Multiple reminders were given, and several offers of a free haircut were extended. Yet, the weekend slowly ticked by, and Solomon's hair remained untouched.

Finally, Solomon was ready for his haircut. Unfortunately, it was nearly 1:00 AM on Monday morning. When he knocked on our neighbor's door to take him up on his offer, the neighbor groggily noted the ungodly hour and refused. Solomon could not understand why our platoon mate, who had offered multiple times to cut his hair throughout the weekend, would now refuse to fulfill his promise just five hours before Monday morning formation. With no other options available to him, Solomon asked if he could at least borrow our platoon mate's hair clippers.

That morning, I was awakened by a hail of laughter coming from the door to our room. Several guys who lived off base with their families had arrived at our platoon area, giddy with excitement to see if Solomon had actually gotten his hair cut or if he had doomed himself to certain death at the hands of our Squad Leader. The truth was oddly somewhere in between.

"C'mon, man. Take off your hat," someone begged.

"Yeah, Solomon, let's see your hair," another voice chimed in.

I could hear Solomon's train noises escaping his mouth in frustration as he yelled at them to go away. Amidst the ruckus, I peeked around my wall lockers to see Solomon standing in front of a gaggle of our platoon mates with a black knit hat covering his head.

The visitors quickly informed me of what had transpired: "Yo, your boy went to ask Hutch to cut his hair at like one in the morning last night, and Hutch told him no. So, Solomon borrowed his clippers and cut his own hair."

This led to another round of laughter and increased pleading for Solomon to remove the hat that now conveniently covered his handiwork. At last, realizing the inevitability of the situation, Solomon removed his cap.

Admittedly, I have never attempted to cut my own hair, so I have no frame of reference for how well I would do in such an undertaking. However, I am quite confident that had I stood in a pitch-black closet at midnight with nothing but a weed whacker, I would have ended up with a far more acceptable coif. Solomon had obviously chosen the lowest possible trimmer setting that still allowed him to retain a trace of hair. Truth be told, the front and sides did not look bad if you were driving past him at 110 miles per hour. Unfortunately, Solomon grossly misjudged his ability to consistently remove hair from the back of his head. What remained was a patchy framework of near-bald spots and untouched tufts of hair. Some patches looked like divots removed from a golf course by a novice golfer, while others resembled rows of corn that had been missed by the tractor during harvest.

Our platoon mates howled with laughter at this spectacle, hugging one another to avoid falling to the ground from the sheer force of their cackling. "Dude, look. He's got racing stripes in the back," one of the guys screamed.

At that time, our Squad Leader arrived and looked into our room to see the source of the commotion. "Jesus Christ," I heard him yell. "Let's go."

Solomon was snatched from the room like a foreign terrorist being plucked from the streets of Morocco by covert operatives in a windowless van. Where he was taken and what punishment he received, I'll never know. But his hair was high and tight by the next time we saw him.

✱✱✱

Like everything else with Solomon, the quiet before the storm seemed to last only for brief periods. Our Squad Leader always seemed just shy of a brain aneurysm with Solomon on his squad. During one morning run, he caught a nose full of Solomon. Finally, someone besides Chuck and I got to experience Solomon's effervescent bundle of olfactory joy that seemed to cling to the walls of our barracks room. Sarge had no patience for the body odor that was now assaulting his nose. He immediately dropped Solomon for push-ups and screamed at him to clean his gray PT uniform by the next day or face the consequences.

Solomon's laziness, filth, and idiocy once again combined for a healthy dose of trouble. The next morning, as we stood in formation, something became readily apparent. While Solomon's PT uniform had historically stunk to high heavens, it was at least somewhat gray in appearance. On this day, however, a platoon of gray PT uniforms surrounded one brown uniform. In a world where we all dressed exactly alike, Solomon stood out like a sore thumb. As we all tried to stifle our laughter at the sight of him, the old Sesame Street song ran in a loop in my head: "One of these things is not like the other. One of these things just doesn't belong."

Our Squad Leader must have been familiar with the song because he immediately picked out the oddball with ease. "Goddammit, Solomon. I told you to wash your uniform," he screamed with a beat-red face.

"I did, Thergeant. I thwear I did," Solomon said as he tried to plead his case.

"Bullshit, Solomon. Everyone else has a gray uniform. Why is yours brown?"

"I washed it, Thergeant. I thwear I washed it." Solomon's protestations did not align with what Sarge's eyes were telling him. The inconsistency seemed to make one specific vein in Sarge's forehead spring to life.

With logic on his side, our Squad Leader made his argument for the mock jury that surrounded Solomon. "Look at these uniforms, Solomon. Gray, gray, gray, gray, BROWN!!!! Why is yours brown?"

Solomon's train noises increased in response to the frustration at not being believed. "Thargeant, I washed my uniform last night. I thwear."

Because his previous arguments seemed to gain no traction, Sarge decided to take a different tack. "Well, what kind of soap did you use? Yours is the only brown uniform in this platoon."

It was a fair question.

Solomon simply stared at the ground in response to Sarge's direct inquiry. He said nothing, and Sarge immediately keyed in on Solomon's silence.

Sarge then seemed to calm down somewhat, as if he were preparing for an answer he wasn't completely sure he wanted to hear. "Solomon?" he asked softly.

Solomon responded with only another frustrated train noise.

"Solomon?" Sarge again asked patiently.

"Yes, Thergeant?"

"What kind of soap did you use to wash your uniform?" At that moment, it was hard to tell what was scarier: Sarge's rage or this newfound calm.

For a brief moment, Solomon seemed to weigh his options before deciding on a full and honest disclosure. "Well, Sergeant. I didn't have any laundry thoap."

"What did you use to wash your uniform, Solomon?" Sarge asked, calmly but forcefully drilling down on the question. Solomon slowly lifted his head to meet his questioner's gaze. "Windex."

The platoon erupted with laughter just as Sarge's head exploded. "Goddammit, Solomon! Get on your face!"

The rest of the platoon gracefully stepped away from the scene.

Looking back, all we could see was Solomon struggling to do push-ups as Sarge yelled in cadence, "1...2...3..." It was truly amazing that Solomon wasn't more muscular.

***

I don't know if the Veterans Administration will allow you to make a disability claim for damage caused by the stress of dealing with an idiot, but I would gladly testify on behalf of our poor Squad Leader. Being an older guy with a completely shaved head, I used to joke with others that he looked like RoboCop when his helmet was removed in the movie. These jokes were kept safely behind his back, as he was a dense package of muscle and not an overly humorous man. He and I had occasionally lifted weights together, so I remained firmly planted on his good side. In fact, the only time I had seen his bad side was after we finished a battle at Dough Boy City.

Dough Boy City was a training facility in West Berlin where infantrymen of the Berlin Brigade practiced urban warfare. We would spend days building fortifications, filling sandbags, and pounding in stakes for razor-sharp concertina wire, all in anticipation of training attacks from opposing forces (OPFOR). The city was comprised of numerous concrete buildings ranging from a single story to four stories. We would practice for hours on end, learning how to defend positions or enter and clear rooms.

During our time at Dough Boy City, it was not uncommon to spend 16-18 hours filling sandbags and fortifying positions for the .50 caliber or M-60 machine gun placements. It was always the same. Everyone would be smoking and joking as we filled and placed sandbag after sandbag. Of course, everyone was well-rested and fully fed when this activity started. However, when it was still going on at three in the morning and people were exhausted and hungry, nerves became frayed, and senses of humor were jettisoned. What was funny at nine in the morning could lead to near fistfights twenty hours later. Eventually, our Squad Leader or Platoon Sergeant would stop by to check our progress and give us the greatest gift of all... sleep. Sleeping in shifts, groups of us would grab our poncho liner blankets and huddle together in tight groups on the bare cement floors of one of the buildings for an hour or two of sleep. From the outside looking in, we must have looked like newborn puppies cuddled together for comfort. In reality, it was simply a way to generate body heat to collectively stay warm.

There are two things I thank the Army for when I look back on those days. First, I have never had a problem falling asleep since joining the military. I have fallen asleep in the soaked woodlands of Germany. I have fallen asleep on the cement floors of Dough Boy City. I have fallen asleep bouncing around in the back of army trucks and various types of helicopters. I have even fallen asleep using an ammunition can, a rock, or a soda can as a pillow. Thanks to the Army, good sleep has always been where you find it. My fellow soldiers and I seemed to have the ability to fall asleep anywhere at a moment's notice because we never knew when we would get the chance to sleep again. Unfortunately, the second gift given to me by the U.S. Army is the fact that

I have no memory of ever feeling well-rested since the day I started Basic Training.

After one early morning training battle, I got a chance to see my Squad Leader's bad side—or should I say his least desirable side. As we finished emptying the hundreds of sandbags we had spent the previous day filling and returned the dirt to the various holes we had dug, I was sent into one of the buildings to retrieve our Squad Leader. Looking from room to room, I yelled out for him, "Hey Sarge. They want you outside."

"Don't come in here," he yelled back.

I'm not sure why I entered the next room despite this warning. Maybe it was the fatigue or the quickly subsiding adrenaline from that morning's tactical exercise. Whatever the reason, I walked in to find him squatting over a metal ammo can as he relieved himself into the empty container with a soft plop.

"Goddammit, Beyer. I told you not to come in here."

"My bad, Sarge," I said as I made a hasty retreat. As I exited the building laughing, I felt compelled to tell my buddies what I had just witnessed. It would have been a sin to keep such information from them. For some reason, I have always been able to tease my bosses, even the surly ones. But I decided to wait a few days before I made light of this experience. As for that ammo can... well, I hope no one ever opened it to see what was simmering inside.

***

This was life in the military. You met a vast array of characters from all over the country. Some became friends, some acquaintances, and some were simply co-workers. Luckily for me, none were enemies. The closest was Solomon, who was later kicked out of the Army after he was caught stealing money from Chuck and me while we slept. Even then, Solomon was more pathetic than evil.

The days and weeks in Berlin seemed to blend into one another. Weekdays started at 6:00 a.m. If you didn't set your alarm, you were simply awakened by a recording of a bugle playing reveille, which crackled to life over the various speakers mounted throughout the McNair Barracks compound. It is a sound that, to this day, still brings a certain degree of anxiety.

Announcements would then be broadcast over the speakers in our building about what PT clothes we were to wear for that morning's exercises. Although we were issued sweatpants, it seemed that someone in the chain of command was particularly averse to keeping our legs warm because we never wore them despite the freezing temperatures. As such, we typically showed up for PT formation in shorts, and on cold days, a sweatshirt if we were lucky. PT typically involved push-ups, sit-ups, various calisthenics, and almost always a run. Longer runs were done through the actual city of Berlin, which was an interesting way to remind us that we were in Europe. We would run in formation through the cobblestone streets, careful to avoid the multitude of bollard posts stationed throughout the city to protect pedestrians and property from vehicle traffic. These were difficult to see because your view was always blocked by the person in front of you. If word was not sent down the line that a bollard post was coming, you were certain to be hit by one in the most sensitive of locations. Hence, they were often referred to as "nutcrackers" or "ball busters."

It was not uncommon for German pedestrians on the street to yell at you to go back to America as we went on these runs. Generally, the comments came from German males who looked astonishingly similar to Mike Myers's portrayal of "Dieter" in the recurring "Sprockets" talk show skits on Saturday Night Live that were popular around that same time. Always dressed in black tights, a matching turtleneck, wire-rimmed glasses, and sporting slicked-back hair, Myers spoke in a thick German accent and acted as a bored and disaffected West German artist. Being heckled by this ilk was always a profound source of irritation for me. Here I was in Berlin, missing home and counting down the days until I could return to the United States. While we were tasked with defending West Berlin from the possibility of a Soviet invasion, we were jeered at by effeminate males who appeared incapable and/or unwilling to defend either themselves or their city.

We experienced similar behavior on public transportation. As soldiers, we were permitted to ride public transportation throughout the city for free. Unfortunately, our buzz cuts and obvious American appearance made us clearly identifiable to those around us. As a result, it was not uncommon for city bus drivers to slam on their brakes as we stood to exit the bus at typical American stops. This would cause soldiers to lose their balance as the bus came to a sudden halt. We all knew this was a passive-aggressive response to our presence, and it was not uncommon for soldiers to shoot a select finger at the bus driver in response. Again, this seemed to be a strange way of thanking those individuals who stood as the last line of defense against Soviet occupation. Perhaps for some citizens of West Berlin, our presence must have already felt like a foreign occupation. So, on those dark mornings when we ran through the city, I braced myself for these types of snide comments and gestures.

After morning PT, we returned to our barracks, showered, dressed for the day, and headed to the chow hall for breakfast. The day's events depended on what block of time we were in. The months were broken down into certain blocks of activity. There were weeks at a time when we would train around the barracks, local ranges, or Dough Boy City to brush up on things like land navigation, marksmanship, and various infantry tactics. There were also weeks when we maintained and cleaned our gear and equipment. But perhaps the most enjoyable block was the weeks we spent in the field. Generally, this involved truck or train trips into West German areas like Wildflecken, Ruhleber, Garmisch, and Sennerlager. Here, we would spend weeks living in tents and training. I always hated the downtime in Berlin, but I loved the field and the training. To me, this is what the Army was supposed to be.

At times, we would train with other units and, at other times, with other countries. On one occasion, a select group of us was given the opportunity to train for two weeks in the field with the Royal Welsh Fusiliers, a line infantry regiment of the British Army originally founded in 1689. This allowed us to experience the military tactics and fire the weaponry of our closest allies. If I thought that the U.S. Army was full of characters, I was woefully unprepared for the uniqueness of this group of English soldiers. Some of the differences were quite comical. For example, unlike the U.S. Army, this group brought their own beer tents into the field with them, resulting in evenings that often sounded like a drunken English pub. The Chaplain's sermons resembled a Benny Hill episode as he comically claimed that while you should not covet your neighbor's wife, it was certainly better than coveting your neighbor's ass. Every morning, we were awakened by yells of "Wakey, wakey, drop your snakey." I was astonished to see that their unit had placed clothing on their targets and filled them with pig guts to replicate the shooting of human flesh, but I was completely perplexed to watch one soldier run downrange and rub some of the blood and guts on his face. They were wild men in the purest sense of the term.

I can also remember sitting next to a Welsh Lieutenant during a period of downtime in our training.

As we sat and ate, he initiated an odd conversation. "You don't care for us much, do you?" he asked.

"I'm sorry, sir?" I responded, looking for clarification.

"You Americans don't care for us much, do you?" he reiterated.

"What do you mean, sir?"

"Well, it seems that America isn't very fond of the English," he continued. Upon hearing this, I felt the need to correct his flawed assertions.

"Sir, we love the Brits. You guys are our closest allies in the world, and here we are training with you now. What would make you think we don't like you?"

He seemed to ponder my information briefly and then noted, "But you seceded from us."

I chuckled at his logic, keeping in mind that he was not only an ally but also an officer deserving of all the respect I could muster. "Well, sir, that was over 200 years ago. I think we're okay now."

He pursed his lips and gave a slight nod of apparent affirmation, as if he had carefully considered and accepted my conclusion. He then smiled and walked away.

At the age of 19, it seemed I had become a statesman building diplomatic bridges in the middle of West Germany. Who would have thought?

The worst part of training with the Brits, however, became apparent at our first meal. Although we were issued mess kits containing a metal plate, pan, and silverware, we never used these items. Instead, hot food was brought to us in the field by truck. We would then form a line and load up paper plates with food. When hot food was not available, we ate from individual pre-packaged field rations known as "Meals Ready to Eat" (or MREs). Based on how we typically received food in the U.S. Army, no one in our group thought to bring our mess kits to train with the Royal Welsh Fusiliers.

At the first meal, we soon realized that the Brits actually used their individual mess kits, meaning no extra utensils were available for us. Realizing this oversight, we ate our first meal with our hands. By the second meal, one of the Americans thankfully scrounged up a plastic fork from some unknown location. Sitting around a table, we each took turns using this highly coveted fork to take a bite of our food before handing it to the person on our left. We then waited for the fork to make its way back to us before taking the next bite. Our desire to eat far outweighed the need for sanitary conditions or a sense of decorum. Though not ideal, this undertaking demonstrated not only ingenuity and teamwork but also the depths of the bonds formed with fellow infantrymen. Luckily, the Brits were able to lay their hands on utensils by the next meal, allowing the poor and woefully unprepared American soldiers to recapture a sense of civility.

***

For some reason, I have no memory of being hot in the field; I was forever cold and wet. As infantrymen, we operated under the adage, "If it ain't rainin', you ain't trainin'." On rainy days, we donned plastic ponchos and continued to march through the woods. Instead of getting our clothes wet from the outside in due to raindrops, we became wet from the inside out from the sweat of exertion. We would snake our way through the woods as we trained, only to be given the word to drop down on our bellies behind our weapons. Being a low-ranking enlisted man, I never knew the reason for our stops, nor did I know how long we would be lying there. This information was rarely passed down the line. We could lie in the woods for a few minutes or for a few hours, but it always seemed to be cold, raining, or snowing when it happened. The incessant combination of being cold, wet, and uninformed ultimately became my biggest motivation for obtaining a college education.

What got me through those miserable days in the field were the little rewards: the promise of a shower in a few days, the excitement of curling up in my sleeping bag to continue reading a Stephen King book when we eventually made it back to our tent, and the hope that we would be eating again soon. Humor often arose from our shared misery. I remember one instance when we stopped in an open field in the countryside of West Germany. It had rained throughout the day, the temperature was in the high thirties, and a wicked breeze whipped through the open clearing on the hill. Everyone was miserably wet and freezing. To lighten the mood, a sergeant friend and I decided to drop our pants to our ankles and engage in a foot race across the field, our soaked boxers whipping in the wind. It was our little way of fighting back against Mother Nature and the discomfort she seemed to incessantly heap upon us. Our antics lifted the mood of the group for a brief period as bets were placed on the winner. I am proud to say that I was the clear winner of the race, and I will deny any claims to the contrary.

Later that day, we eventually marched our way to the very outskirts of humanity and civilization. Our return to civilization was marked by an unusually placed commercial food truck in the middle of nowhere. Having been in the field for days, no one had a wallet. Still, my sergeant friend and I managed to scrounge up a couple of bucks and jumped in line with a few others who had some loose currency. The aroma emanating from the food truck was intoxicating, and the grimy group of us standing in line seemed to salivate in unison. Together, Sarge and I could afford one burger, and we handed off the remaining change to others in the group who were desperate for food. Walking back to our position, Sarge and I took turns biting from the burger as we passed it back and forth. It certainly was not how either of us would have preferred to eat a hamburger, but desperate times called for desperate measures. What seems repulsive now as I write this seemed both ingenious and humanizing then.

***

When we returned home from the field, I often felt bored. The downtime and weekends tended to drag on endlessly. Many of the guys were drawn to the bars to drink or to the Berlin discotheques to chase German girls who seemed overly eager to follow them home to the United States. Some even frequented the part of town known as "Sixty Mark Strasse." Translated into English, "Sixty Dollar Street" offered a different type of German woman who was not necessarily looking to marry a lonely American soldier. Luckily, my core group of friends was much more laid-back. Since the movies on base cycled every day or two, we went to the movies constantly. We'd also work out, visit the Post Exchange (PX) to shop, go out to nice dinners in downtown Berlin, or attend concerts when American acts came to perform. We even had the chance to see Bob Hope's performance for the troops at Tempelhof Airport in May 1990. In August of that same year, several of us traveled to see the Rams play the Chiefs in the American Bowl at the Olympic Stadium in Berlin. This opportunity to see live NFL football was a welcome reprieve from the German language and culture that surrounded us.

In November 1990, during our morning formation, we were informed by our platoon sergeant that an American movie company would be filming a World War II movie in Berlin. The producers were looking for extras to play German soldiers in the film and would pay $80 to anyone interested in participating. A handful of us jumped at the chance. How often do you get to be an extra in a Hollywood movie?

We made our way to the set and learned that the movie was called "Shining Through," starring Michael Douglas, Melanie Griffith, and Liam Neeson. Our role was to portray German soldiers lining the streets and holding back the crowd as a parade of Hitler Youth marched down the cobblestone streets. We were then directed to a large room filled with props where they outfitted us with uniforms, helmets, boots, and rifles. Upon entering the set, I was amazed at how fake and small everything seemed. Large red Nazi banners hung from artificial-looking building fronts, and the crowd appeared to consist of a relatively small number of individuals dressed in 1940s-era German clothing.

My friends and I stood on the curb at attention with our rifles slung over our shoulders. Then, a small group of children dressed as Hitler Youth banged on drums and held trumpets to their lips as they marched past us. Once that was done, they repeated the process over and over again as the cameras rolled. Being November, it was freezing yet again. Our thin wool uniforms and ill-fitting boots proved no match for the frigid wind that howled down the parade route. My backbone ached as I tried to hold back my shivering.

In addition to the unrelenting cold, what stands out in my memory is how unimpressive everything seemed and the redundancy associated with filming the scene repeatedly. It ended up being a much longer day than any of us had expected. However, the greatest source of irritation was the young child star who was part of the Hitler Youth parade. Each time he reached the end of the parade route, a beautiful woman would wrap him in the most enormous fur coat I have ever seen and then walk him back to the beginning to reshoot the scene. Here we were standing at attention, the wind beating against us, while this 12-year-old, who seemed both condescending and unappreciative of his star treatment, was immediately draped in fur when the word "cut" was yelled across the set. Despite the ire the boy drew from our group of extras, the experience was memorable, the pictures we took were one of a kind, and we each walked out with eighty bucks in cash. Not bad for a day's work.

Through cycles of being cold in the field and warm back in the barracks, as well as the unique experiences we were afforded in Berlin, time was ticking by. I had gotten into a good rhythm, and friendships were growing. I had quickly been promoted from Private (E-1) to Private (E-2) to Private First Class (E-3), and then to Specialist (E-4). Things were moving along, and I was living on a steady diet of "Just keep your head down – things are rolling." Unfortunately, change is inevitable, and both the world and the Berlin Brigade were about to experience a profound change.

6

THE WORLD CHANGES

On August 2, 1990, Iraq invaded its neighboring country of Kuwait, and the name of Saddam Hussein became prominent in nightly news broadcasts. Such outright aggression seemed to galvanize the world, and the United States, along with a coalition of 42 other countries, began a military buildup along the Iraqi/Saudi Arabian border. This military buildup continued until January 1991 and came to be known as Operation Desert Shield. As more and more U.S. troops deployed to the area, the involvement of the Berlin Brigade in these tensions became a constant topic of discussion within our unit. Many of the rank and file assumed that our unit would likely not be called upon because the U.S. could not afford to leave the border between West Berlin and East Berlin unguarded. Only time would tell.

Around this same time, word spread throughout the Berlin Brigade that a soldier from the 6th Battalion had been shot and killed during a recent live-fire exercise. This sad revelation, combined with Iraq's incursion into Kuwait days earlier, served as a reminder of the gravity of what we were doing in the military and what we had all signed up for. We were not soldiers on a movie set; this was not training. War was on the horizon.

Rumors also began to swirl around the 4th Battalion during this time period. With the Berlin Wall slowly being disassembled piece by piece and the reunification of the once-divided country of Germany becoming a reality, questions started to arise about the need for such a robust American military presence in Berlin. Similarly, it was reported that the buildings on McNair Barracks would be repurposed to house former East German citizens. As such, suggestions that the 4th Battalion was being targeted for deactivation became a routine topic of discussion. Speculations soon followed. Some claimed to have heard that our battalion would be absorbed by the 4th Infantry Division at Fort Carson, Colorado. Others claimed to have it on good authority that we would become part of the 101st Airborne Division at Fort Campbell, Kentucky. Either option was a source of great excitement for me, as it meant I would hopefully be reassigned to a stateside location. This could greatly impact my decision about separating from the Army.

This situation reminded me of why you should never gamble and why you should never believe rumors. By December 1990, we learned that 4th Battalion had been selected for deactivation. With this news came the deflating realization that I would not be reassigned to a unit in the United States. Instead, many of us would simply pack up our belongings and walk two blocks down the street to 6th Battalion for new assignments. This news was terribly disappointing because the hope of a U.S. assignment had quickly and assuredly been pulled out from under me. Simply put, I would be spending the rest of my military service in Berlin.

***

The start of the new year in January 1991 brought expected news. As we stood in formation in front of 4th Battalion in the early morning hours of January 17, 1991, we were informed that Operation Desert Shield had become Operation Desert Storm. More specifically, we were told that the first wave of American aircraft had begun targeting Iraqi military installations. War had begun. This brought an uneasy mix of intense pride and well-wishes for our military comrades, along with concern for what this meant for me and my fellow infantrymen of the Berlin Brigade. It was then explained that 200 volunteers from our neighboring 6th Battalion—my soon-to-be new home—were being sought to serve as truck drivers in this new operation. It appeared that war was hitting much closer to home than originally anticipated.

The start of America's new war in the Gulf was also felt in the reactions of many Berliners. Protests immediately began outside our barracks and other U.S. facilities in the city. Protesters chanted and carried signs that read "Klein Krieg Im Gulf." Four years of high school German allowed me to translate this as "No War in the Gulf." What was particularly grating to my nerves was their heavily accented renditions of John Lennon's "Give Peace a Chance." As a young American service member, it all seemed so clichéd. It also appeared quite paradoxical considering the fathers and grandfathers of these same protesters had invaded numerous European countries just a few decades earlier during World War II. At the time, I was left wondering whether they supported one country invading another or were against those who fought back against such aggression. I was also shocked to see how these ostensible purveyors of peace rushed the Berlin Brigade Headquarters, necessitating the closing of stores and the use of tanks to block access to U.S. installations and American schools. Unlike American police, protesting did not seem to be as readily tolerated by the German Polizei, who delivered swift and certain beatings to those protesters who became too militant. Thankfully, the fallout over the start of Desert Storm was short-lived as U.S. and allied forces quickly and decisively broke the backs of the Iraqi military in just 100 hours.

***

By March 1991, the time had come for those of us being reassigned to 6th Battalion to walk down the street and receive our new platoon assignments. This proved to be a difficult time because not only was my family of the last year being broken up, but I was also being reassigned to an HHC (Headquarters and Headquarters Company) unit. Unlike infantry units that prepare for combat, soldiers in HHC detachments provide administrative and tactical support. More specifically, it was explained to me that I would be reassigned as a truck driver. This news devastated me.

While the Army was not shaping up to be my lifelong career, I was most proud of the fact that I was an infantryman. We had derogatory terms for the support personnel who were not trained to be on the front lines or in direct combat. We called them disparaging names like "Pogue" or "REMF" (a derogatory acronym standing for Rear-Echelon... well, you can guess the rest). The one source of pride I had left was now being taken from me.

Upon moving to my new unit, I had to meet a whole new group of guys. Because none of them were infantrymen, the behavior, attitude, and general atmosphere were completely different. They were all truck drivers. That was it. That was the extent of their skills. However, before I cast aspersions upon them, it was important to remember that I was not superior to them. In fact, I had no idea how to drive a stick shift at that time. So, from that standpoint, they already had a leg up on me. Out of a sense of desperation, I made my way to the First Sergeant's office, the senior non-commissioned officer for the unit. After I introduced myself, I pleaded with him to assign me to one of the infantry platoons.

He said no.

I then explained that I had enlisted in the Army to be an infantryman.

He replied that I had enlisted in the Army to do what I was told.

In a last-ditch effort, I explained that I didn't even know how to drive a manual transmission.

He then kicked me out of his office with four short words: "You'll figure it out."

And that was it. I was now a truck driver.

★★★

It has often been said that God never closes a door without opening a window. This proved to be the case in my new assignment. Although I was being assigned to the Support Platoon in Bravo Company with the other truck drivers, it appeared that my new duty would be slightly, yet thankfully, a bit more demanding. I would actually work as an ammunition specialist. Of course, that made perfect sense. Although I now carried the rank of Specialist, I had no specialization whatsoever regarding ammunition beyond the rounds I placed in my assigned infantry weapons. But I quickly learned that what you're called and what you do are often two different things in the Army. Believe me, I was no specialist. Nor did my duties require the "Specialist" qualifier. I simply drove to and from the ammunition supply points and storage locations to count, receive, document, and distribute the ammunition requested by the infantry units.

With this new assignment, I lost the close connections shared among infantry units. My new platoon was just a group of guys who were loosely affiliated with one another. Luckily, I spent most of my initial months on the job driving around with another guy named Brad (a general source of confusion) as we listened over and over again to Eddie Money's greatest hits on a boombox bungee-corded between our headrests. We would arrive at a range or training location, hand out crates of ammunition, document the exchanges, and move on to the next stop. While I bemoaned the loss of my old assignment, I soon realized the new assignment offered a number of perks. The amount of time spent in the cold and wet weather was drastically decreased. If things got too miserable, we sat in the warm truck while the infantry guys suffered. In the field, we often sat in warm buildings, passing the time by watching movies, reading books, or listening to music while my former grunt buddies wallowed in the same misery that I had come to detest. With trucks at our disposal, we ate when and where we wanted instead of receiving orders about when we could chow down on our prepackaged MREs.

For many, this new life might be perceived as the military's equivalent of winning the lottery. Unfortunately for me, it also brought a great deal of guilt. As I dropped off ammo during field exercises, I would occasionally run into my former 4th Battalion platoon mates. I would jump out of the truck, warm, clean, and in dry clothing, only to be greeted by my old pals, who were cold, wet, and smelly, their faces smeared with a combination of grime and camouflage paint. They would engage in snarky comments about how I had turned into a Pogue and how nice it must be to be warm and dry. I would return their wisecracks with witty ammunition of my own, but deep down, I felt spoiled and traitorous. It was difficult to enjoy the fringe benefits of a job I didn't ask for while simultaneously hating my exclusion from the shared suffering of my friends. I attempted to justify it by telling myself that I did everything I could to stay in an infantry unit.

The First Sergeant was correct, however: I did learn to drive a stick shift. In reality, I may have bent the truth a bit in claiming to have no knowledge of a manual transmission. Because of my parents' bankruptcy, there was a time when my father was relegated to driving an old Plymouth Citation that not only had a manual transmission but also lacked power steering. Truth be told, aside from the difference in height, driving his Citation was not that far off from driving an army truck.

My second introduction to the stick shift occurred with the "Deuce-and-a-Half." First known as the CCKW 6X6 during

World War II, its nickname came from its ability to carry 2 ½ tons of material both on and off-road. In the 1950s, it was replaced by the M35, which was used throughout the Korean and Vietnam wars. Though powerful and capable, it was not a vehicle built for comfort or speed. The pads used for the seat and backrests fell somewhere between a lawn chair cushion and a computer mouse pad. Shifting the mighty beast into gear felt like trying to ram a wheelchair through a subway turnstile. Eventually, you would get it in, but not without a fight.

One of my first trips driving a Deuce-and-a-Half involved taking a load of soldiers to the Grunewald. The Grunewald is a forested area of more than 7,400 acres just west of Berlin. I had previously spent countless hours in the Grunewald training and practicing infantry tactics. What was interesting was the fact that, because it was a public forest, it was not uncommon to see park benches, walkers, joggers, or even young parents pushing baby strollers in certain locations. Dressed in camouflage uniforms and walking around the woods, we would sometimes stumble across an elderly couple holding hands. It always amazed me that this did not lead to jumps, screams, or any identifiable level of concern from these German citizens. I often wondered how the responses would differ in America if foreign soldiers crawled out of the woods in New York's Central Park and came across a woman pushing a baby buggy.

The Grunewald was also the location of my introductory hazing when I first arrived at the 4th Battalion. As soon as I reached my first duty station, I heard that, as a newcomer to the platoon, I could expect to be welcomed in a distinct and individualized ceremony. To keep the story rated PG, I'll refer to this initiation as being "tree plucked." This unique welcome involved my new platoon mates pummeling the newcomer, lifting him by his arms and legs, and then taking him to the nearest tree. Once the right tree was selected, the guys holding the feet of the newcomer would pull his legs apart so that he had one leg on either side of the tree. Then, as a group, they would pull the newcomer's legs and push his upper body in unison, smashing his groin repeatedly into the tree trunk. Hence the term "tree plucking"

I remember one particular training day when we broke into separate squads to run through individual squad tactics. At the time, my squad leader was a young black Staff Sergeant who fancied himself a bit of a preacher. During a break, as we lay in a rough circle on the ground, Sarge read aloud a selected passage from a Bible he carried with him. It was actually a warming moment. Still, something seemed amiss. Having a profound fear of the unknown and being one to address challenges head-on, I decided to raise my hand and ask Sarge a question as he finished reading. He raised his chin, signaling for me to ask my question.

"Sarge, am I going to get tree plucked? Because if I am, I would rather be tree plucked by my squad than by the entire platoon."

While my request may have sounded strange, it was a strategic one. A beating from eight or ten guys was surely better than a beating from forty.

Sarge listened to my question, tipped his head to the side as if considering my rationale, and then slowly closed his Bible. He looked at me and stated, "Well Beyer, just ask and you shall receive, sayeth the Lord."

At that moment, I knew it was game on. Instincts kicked in. My sympathetic nervous system began pumping blood, sweat, and oxygen to the relevant parts of my body, and I did what any normal person would do: I took off running. My dash through the woods was short, as I was quickly surrounded by my squad mates who flanked me like a pack of velociraptors on the hunt. I was then tackled and pummeled as a barrage of fists sought out the parts of my body not protected by my arms. Those not involved in landing blows began grasping for my arms and legs in an attempt to lift me off the ground.

As the grappling continued, I realized that my roommate Chuck was laughing as he landed blow after blow on my legs. I recalled that Chuck had previously informed me he had never received his tree plucking from the platoon. This seemed antithetical to the joy he was experiencing as he participated in mine.

"Yo, Chuck never got tree plucked either," I yelled out in the chaos. The grin on Chuck's face drained like a suddenly unclogged bathroom sink.

Standing up and backing away from the site of my beating, Chuck held up his hands in submission, panic on his face. "Wait a minute, guys," he pleaded. "I have back problems." Chuck then bolted from the scene.

Like zombies who had found a fresh body to gnaw on, some of the squad members left me behind and took off after the fleeing Navajo with reported back problems.

"Go get yours, Chucky boy," I thought to myself.

The remainder of the squad lifted me off the ground, found a neighboring tree, and began ramming my nether regions into the bark. Thankfully, the tree they selected was a tad too wide, which meant direct contact between the tree and my unmentionables was slightly mitigated. I provided them with obligatory yells to quell their quest for pain and agony, and they soon dropped me. As I lay sprawled beneath the tree, basking in the loss of my forest virginity, I could hear Chuck's screams a short distance away. Then, someone came up with the idea of giving Solomon a fresh tree plucking.

He lisped and honked out nasally yelps as the group continued their behavior on a new target. Unfortunately for Solomon, he had already received numerous tree pluckings, as well as fire hydrant and corner-of-building pluckings in Dough Boy City. Even more problematic for him was the fact that the tree selected for him that day was the width of a stop sign post. This all but ensured that Solomon's groin and the tree made direct and painful contact. A fruit basket, a free lunch at Applebee's, a cake at the office... I can think of many ways to welcome a new co-worker, but none of them involved genital torture.

***

While the tree plucking was my infantry introduction to the Grunewald, driving a platoon of infantry soldiers there for land navigation training was my truck driving introduction. I followed two other trucks through Berlin as we made our way to the forest. My shifting was not quite up to par, as could be discerned by the yells coming from the troops in the back of the truck. I tried telling everyone that truck driving was not my forte, but no one listened. As far as I was concerned, if the guys in the back were experiencing a rough ride, they could thank the First Sergeant. After all, he was the one who told me I would figure out how to drive these clunky vehicles. Eventually, we all made it to the Grunewald, with my driving improving only modestly en route.

Everyone jumped out and embarked on the land navigation course. This involved using a compass and written directions. For example, the directions might say to head out on an azimuth of 135 degrees for 800 meters. This meant that we were to hold the compass in front of us and turn until we were facing 135 degrees. We would then walk in that direction for 800 meters. Everyone had previously learned their pace count—in other words, how many left steps it would take to reach 100 meters. My pace count was 62. So, as I walked following the 135-degree azimuth, I counted every time my left foot landed. When I reached 62, I knew that I had walked 100 meters and had 700 more to go. When you eventually reached the destination, you looked for a small post in the ground that included a number and letter combination. You would write this combination on your printed directions to verify that you had reached the correct point. Because you were walking through the woods and over various types of terrain, keeping a straight line and consistent pace count often became challenging. As a result, the post was not always easily located. Since we all started at different locations and had different directions, it was not uncommon to pass one of your fellow soldiers, who might point you in the right direction as they had just found the same post that you were now looking for.

On this particular trip, I found my last post and documented it on my sheet.Unfortunately, I was not exactly sure how to get back to the trucks from that last location.

In life, we all have strengths and weaknesses. Some people excel at math but struggle with writing. Others have beautiful singing voices but couldn't throw a baseball if promised a small fortune. I have come to realize that these weaknesses only become problematic when you fail to admit them to yourself. Perhaps my most profound weakness is my complete and utter lack of a sense of direction. Sadly, this weakness seems to run through my bloodline. In fact, I have joked over the years that if the Beyer family crest or coat of arms contains any German script, it would surely translate to read, "Where the hell are we?"

With only a vague sense of where I was going, I started walking and walking and walking. The sun was beginning to set as I continued on my way. My concern was only outmatched by my burning frustration. I encountered no other soldiers, which was both a positive and a negative. I was relieved that no one could witness me wandering around the Grunewald, lost. This spared me from becoming the subject of a story about a soldier who had to be rescued from his own failed internal compass, along with all the teasing that would accompany it. I told myself those were positives. The downside was that, since I had driven a group of soldiers out, they must be waiting for me to return so they could be driven back to the barracks. The stress of everyone waiting for me sent my worries into overdrive. Fortunately, since the movie "Home Alone" had not yet been created, I was thankfully not operating under the fear of being left behind by the others.

After a couple of hours of aimless wandering, I finally returned to our rally point. It was now dark, and I was greeted by a solitary truck sitting lifelessly in the parking lot.

I assumed everyone must have tired of waiting for me and crammed into the other two vehicles to depart. Fortunately, they left me a truck with the keys in the ignition. At that moment, I didn't know whether to be grateful that no one was around to witness my shame or angry that they had left me all alone without any sign of concern. I jumped into the truck, turned the key, and listened as the diesel engine of the old relic rattled to life. As I forced the stick shift into first gear, I was met with a new yet familiar fear: not only did I lack a sense of direction in the Grunewald, but I also had no sense of direction on the streets of Berlin.

I quickly learned that despite having a truck at my disposal, I was certainly not home free. As I hit the roadways with no map and no concept that something called GPS would become readily available in the years to come, I soon realized I was in trouble. Some things looked familiar, but the darkness caused what little landmarks there were to appear significantly different. Wrong turn after wrong turn, I found I had simply exchanged wandering around aimlessly on foot for wandering around aimlessly by truck. Some of these wrong turns led me onto extremely narrow cobblestone streets lined with parked cars on both sides. It became a matter of simple physics: when a truck that is too wide is on a street that is too narrow, something has to give. Unfortunately, that breaking point was the side mirrors of numerous parked cars. As I heard one side mirror after another break off in my wake, all I could think was, "Hey First Sergeant, I told you I couldn't do this."

Eventually, like in the Grunewald, I made my way back to the motor pool. I parked my big olive drab dinosaur of a truck in a spot and walked back to the barracks. I braced myself for the ridicule that was bound to follow. Strangely enough, no jokes were cracked, and no comments were ever made about the situation. God works in mysterious ways. Through the whole ordeal, I had learned how to drive these enormous trucks with quirky manual transmissions after all. I had become so preoccupied with finding my way back to the barracks that I didn't realize I had been learning how to drive a stick shift in the process. Better yet, I likely made the local body shop owner in Berlin a rich man as well. It was a win-win.

7
TURKEY

During my new assignment in 6th Battalion, I began to form new relationships with a whole new group of characters from a whole new set of states. Luckily, two infantry buddies from 4th Battalion accompanied me to 6th Battalion. Like me, they had also signed up for the two-year Infantry special at the time and were equally looking forward to the end of their Army service. Ray was a Bruce Springsteen aficionado from Delaware who shared my sense of humor and penchant for quoting movies. We would hang out for hours, feeding off one another's jokes. It was not until years later that I came to realize our relationship was not unlike that of Jerry Seinfeld and George Costanza. I will lay claim to the role of Jerry, as I am the one telling the story and I was a bit taller than Ray. Like the sitcom 'Seinfeld,' our relationship was a relationship about nothing. We talked about everything and nothing at the same time. We pontificated on everything and accomplished nothing. Yet every discussion centered around one thing: trying to make the other one laugh. Had TikTok existed at the time, we surely would have created a rich collection of material that would have undoubtedly been viewed by dozens of people worldwide.

While Ray and I had grown up roughly an hour away from each other, my other friend Ron and I shared no similarities whatsoever. Though he lived in Miami at the time of his enlistment, he was actually born in Nicaragua. As a young boy, he experienced the Nicaraguan Revolution, in which the Sandinista National Liberation Front overthrew the government in 1979. Since Ron's father had ties to the existing Nicaraguan government, the armed insurrection of the Sandinistas placed his family at great risk. Ron explained how he and his siblings were rushed from school and evacuated from the area with their family by helicopter. Eventually, they resettled in Miami, where they began a new life.

Ron's heritage, his ability to speak fluent Spanish, and his life in a warm, magical place called Miami made him extremely interesting to me. When watching action movies with Hispanic characters, I would lean over in the theater, and he would automatically provide translation. He taught me a few Spanish phrases—some appropriate for general use and others not. I could ask him in Spanish how he was doing and if he was ready to go to lunch at the mess hall. When others would hear this exchange, they would exclaim in surprise, "Beyer, I didn't know you could speak Spanish!" I would then rattle off an incomprehensible language that vaguely sounded like Spanish, and Ron would respond to me in actual Spanish, as if he understood everything I had just babbled. People would walk away astonished at my linguistic abilities while Ron and I just laughed, keeping my Spanish ignorance as a joke between us.

Our differences in backgrounds also became a source of good-natured ribbing. Ron would often refer to me as

"Gringo." Arguments would also erupt over the abilities of the Dolphins versus the Eagles or the 76ers versus the Heat. Looking back on my time in the military, it is sad to see how much of America's efforts at political correctness have actually robbed its citizens of humor and bonding. In the Army, everything was fair game when it came to joke-cracking. Race, color, creed, religion, state of origin, military occupational specialty—everything was on the table. No one ever took offense to this type of banter. In fact, I have no recollections of anyone ever holding ill will toward anyone else in the unit, and I certainly don't remember fistfights breaking out. Perhaps it was because, if nothing else, we could at least connect on the fact that we were Americans and soldiers. We all had that in common. What race we were, where we came from—everything after that was unimportant window dressing. If anything, these differences made each person interesting and unique rather than an assumed part of a preordained group of victims and oppressors.

In cities like Norristown, most people were born and raised in your hometown. A new kid in your class from a different school district seemed exotic. It was rare to meet people from a different state, and you certainly didn't meet Germans, Brits, or Nicaraguans. In Norristown, everyone spoke the same way. Everyone knew about the Shore, hoagies, and water ice. Everyone pronounced "water" as "wooder." No one asked, "Have you eaten yet?" They simply slurred out the question, "Djeetyet?" and the person you were talking to replied, "No, Djou?" If you were talking to more than one person, you referred to them as "Youse." It was a shared common language and a shared cultural background. But in the Army, with its endless ranks of soldiers from all over the United States, you met people who had no idea what you were talking about. If you cared enough to ask, you could learn about what it was like to grow up in Miami, Alaska, or Southern California. Then, if you became friends with those people, you teased them about their backgrounds as you tried to convince them why yours was superior. It was a way of acknowledging differences, creating healthy competition, and marking the pride you had in your own unique upbringing and life experiences. It was completely normal and, unlike today, it actually bonded guys instead of dividing them. Maybe one day, American citizens can resurrect these types of thick-skinned and good-natured relationships with one another.

***

After a few months of acclimating to my new unit and the characters that came with it, word began to circulate about an upcoming deployment. It appeared that the Gulf War had left some unfinished business. The rumor mill surrounding this potential deployment was activated, and educated guesses were tossed from ear to ear, whether you wanted to hear them or not. Then, in July of 1991, the gossip and hearsay were put to rest." Bravo and HHC Companies of the 6th Battalion, 502nd Infantry Regiment, along with select elements of the 42nd Engineer Company, were informed that they would become Task Force 6-502nd and deploy to Turkey as part of Operation Provide Comfort II. As it was explained to us, the United States and other countries of the

Gulf War coalition agreed to engage in a military operation to defend and provide humanitarian aid to the Kurdish refugees fleeing northern Iraq in the wake of Operation Desert Storm. It was estimated that we would be deployed to Turkey for between three and six months. We were permitted to tell our families that we would be deployed, but for now, we could not disclose our destination.

Over the next few days, we gathered our equipment and prepared for our new mission. I called home to inform my parents about my deployment. The lack of available information heightened their concerns, and I promised to share more details as they became available. For me, another question also arose: since I was about five months away from the end of my term of service, was it possible that I would be involuntarily extended as part of this deployment? Three to six months was the projection, but what if things went longer? I strategically pushed this question into the back of my mind. I would have plenty of time to worry about it later.

After a few days of frantic preparation, seventy members of my unit boarded an enormous Air Force C-5 Galaxy. While I had concerns for my physical safety, especially given the glaring lack of details provided to us, I was also excited. This was what it was all about. This was what I had signed up for. The incessant training would finally be put to good use. The theoretical was about to become actual. As our mental and physical preparations were starting to kick in, so too was the ineptitude of the federal government.

After sitting on the runway for nearly two hours, stirring in our broth of apprehension and eagerness, we were ordered off the plane. As we stood in formation with all our gear, we were told that the politicians were unable to obtain the necessary authority for us to land in Turkey. It felt like we had made the laborious ascent of a roller coaster, each of us readying ourselves for the exhilarating drop that follows—only no drop came. All the nervousness and anticipation simply dissolved into an ineffectual bureaucratic fizzle.

We were then instructed to return to our barracks and remain on a two-hour recall. In other words, we were told to go about our lives, but be ready to return to this same spot in two hours once the word went out. More colloquially, we were told to "standby to standby." It seems that the orders to "hurry up and wait" are the lifeblood of federal bureaucracies. It is the grease that lubricates the slow, yet powerful, wheels of America's largest institutions. And truth be told, I have always loathed it. Do I have time to eat? Should I sleep? Do I have time for a shower? Have you heard anything? These are the questions that circulate when you are asked to dance on the head of a pin while upper management attempts to rectify their cranial-rectal inversion. So, for five days, we lived in this anticipatory stew until finally, word was received: "Let's go."

This time, the flight was ready to proceed. On July 19, 1991, we departed Berlin. We landed at Rhein-Main Air Force Base in Frankfurt, Germany, not long thereafter. We were informed that we needed to refuel, which seemed odd to me. Apparently, the pilots must operate this giant aircraft like I used to drive my old Dodge Dart: don't worry about the fuel level; the little red light will tell you when it's time to fill her up.

When we arrived, the runway was swarmed with flashing fire trucks, and we were ordered to deplane. Clearly, this was not a routine refueling. Had we come close to crashing? Were firefighters anticipating the arrival of a fiery fuselage? Of course, no additional information was provided to help explain the situation. Instead, we sat around for hours, wondering what the hell was going on and questioning the dependability of the large military aircraft we had just flown in on. Eventually, we were ordered back onto the very same plane, and we departed. Was it safe? Was something in desperate need of repair? Of course, there were no answers to our nagging questions, just a healthy dose of "Shut up and get on board, soldier." Only time would tell if our next landing would be more or less eventful.

***

On the morning of July 20, 1991, we landed safely and in a much-appreciated, unexciting manner at Incirlik Air Force Base in south-central Turkey. As the doors opened and we made our way onto the tarmac, one thing was clear: we were no longer in Germany. The palm trees that dotted the surrounding area were the first clue that we were no longer in Western Europe. However, it was the heat that drove the point home. It seemed to hit you in the face like being on the receiving end of a major league ball player's home run swing. After what felt like 18 months of being cold, the heat was not an unpleasant welcome.

We were then transported to what was essentially a tent city established within the confines of the base. We staged in this area for four days, staving off boredom and watching occasional softball games at a neighboring field. Yet again, we hurried to get here and were then ordered to wait. Although we were anxious to get to our final location, word trickled down of a soldier being killed by some sort of explosion not far from where we were heading. Unlike the later wars in Iraq and Afghanistan, U.S. fatalities in Operation Desert Storm were few and far between. To hear word of the death of a U.S. servicemember was a somber reminder that our impending operation was not a training exercise.

On the fifth day, we boarded multiple charter buses for the 14-hour drive to our final destination. As we headed dead east, the large windows of the bus offered an expansive view of essentially nothing. The countryside was both spectacular and, at the same time, horrible. It seemed as if God had painted this particular part of the world with just two colors: gray and beige. Our journey took us through a constant loop of either bleak, craggy mountains or endless barren stretches of dry, cracked earth. For hour after hour, the landscape blended into a blur of oatmeal-colored emptiness. We passed through small towns with decrepit stone homes. Some were built into the mountainside; others seemed to grow out of the cracked earth. Some were nothing more than rudimentary tents and lean-tos. None of them seemed to have windows to protect the occupants from the sun, which bore down on them relentlessly. Pack mules, goats, sheep, and cows meandered between the homes and people without concern or destination.

Back in the States, as I drove along sturdy highways, I marveled at the small, tattered homes lining the Pennsylvania Turnpike. I often wondered how some people lived. These thoughts were magnified exponentially by the images I took in during my bus trip through southern

Turkey. I watched dusty children run around, kicking up even more dust in their wake. Old men sat and stared as our buses, packed with American troops, drove by. Rarely were women present; perhaps they were inside preparing meals or engaged in a futile battle to keep the interiors free of dirt. I remember one small boy standing next to his father as we passed. With a sideways glance, he stepped back so his father would not see him raise his tiny fist at us in what I assumed was a sign of solidarity. This continued for hours as we traversed the bleak landscape on our way to our final destination.

At one point, the buses stopped at a rest area. We clamored off the buses to stretch our legs and share our thoughts about what we had seen through the windows. As we talked and stretched, I observed a Turkish man walk from behind a building carrying a backpack sprayer with a running motor. From the attached plastic tube in his hand, he methodically dispensed gray smoke behind us. Perhaps it was my own paranoia at being in a strange land or a noticeable helping of PTSD stirring up memories of gas training at Fort Benning, but the sight of the smoke sent me rushing back into the bus to retrieve my gas mask. I was astonished to see that none of my fellow soldiers followed my lead. In fact, none of them seemed remotely concerned about this dark-complected stranger who was permeating our area with smoke. Granted, the majority of these soldiers were not infantrymen, but did they not have any inherent sense of operational security or at least a desire for self-preservation? As I located my gas mask carrier and prepared for the donning procedure we had practiced repeatedly at Fort Benning, the reality of the situation finally caught up to my instincts. The man was simply spraying for mosquitoes. I had certainly never seen this activity in Norristown, and I am not sure how the thought finally dawned on me, but with a soft chuckle to myself, I realized my own idiocy. Fortunately, none of the others had observed my rash behavior, and thanks to the good Lord above, I did not exit the bus wearing my gas mask. That surely would have made me a target for future comical torture.

***

We finally arrived at our new home on the outskirts of Silopi, Turkey. The city of Silopi is located just a few miles from the borders of both Iraq and Syria. At that time, the population of the city was roughly 50,000 people, though the term "city" is somewhat misleading. It was not a large, sprawling metropolitan area from what I could tell, and our location was little more than an expanse of flat desert. When we arrived, the temperature was 119 degrees, which seemed to suck the air from your lungs when you exited the bus. The oppressive heat was matched only by the grubby landscape of our new home.

It appeared that our living quarters were still a work in progress. Dirt-colored, or what some might call khaki-colored, tents were crammed together and scattered across acres of flat, arid earth, protected from outside interference by coiled strands of concertina wire. Dust kicked up by Humvee tires and footfalls seemed to be sucked toward the baking sun. Soldiers already on the scene worked like bees in a hive as they readied the new environment for habitation. Piles of wood and garbage were left behind as they moved about the area. Bathroom facilities consisted of wooden shacks. A call for number one led you to a wooden shack with a long, slanted trough. It was a urinal ramp that allowed for a constant flow of pee from the soldiers uphill as it gathered in some unknown location that I hoped I would never have to learn about.

Should you find yourself in need of going number two, you were directed to another wooden shack. As I opened the door to reconnoiter where I would need to go when the time came, I was graced with a disheartening reality. Inside this "shit shack" was a large elevated box that ran the length of the interior. On top of the box were four holes, approximately two feet apart, encircled by a toilet seat bolted to the box. With no partition between them, I realized that when the inevitable occurred, I would have to sit shoulder-to-shoulder with another soldier who shared the same gastrointestinal clock. For just a moment, I wondered if I could hold it for the next three to six months.

It is funny how we are all capable of adapting to our surroundings. While my inherent modesty and desire for privacy begged for an option other than the shit shack, just a few short days were all that was required to catapult any humility or shyness into the surrounding desert. Proof of this was hammered home one day when I found myself having to respond to nature's call.

At that time in the United States, the story of a cannibalistic serial killer in Milwaukee named Jeffrey Dahmer was just beginning to break. The story was covered in the military's Stars and Stripes newspaper, which was made available to us. Fascinated by the gruesome investigation and the details that were slowly emerging, I grabbed a copy of the paper and headed to the shack. While just days earlier I had felt panicked about the bathroom situation, I now found myself perched on the wooden box with three other soldiers as I read the paper. Any remaining modesty had plummeted to the depths of wherever our last digested meals were now headed. To make matters worse, a Turkish woman tasked with cleaning the shack opened the door, exposing us to the outside world. After mumbling some incomprehensible words, the old woman began mopping the floor as we all sat there going to the bathroom. To make things easier for her, we each rhythmically raised and lowered our feet with each pass of her mop. It was at that moment that I realized there exists a discernible sense of empowerment when you no longer care about what other people think.

***

Outside of our rudimentary encampment, the seeds of capitalism had begun to grow. Silopi residents had set up stands where they sold everything from sandals to ornate Turkish rugs to Zippo lighters. This became our new shopping mall. As you walked around, you were bombarded with salespeople who pestered you to stop and take a look at the varied quality items they offered for purchase. Small Turkish children would kick dirt onto your boots and then beg to shine them for a small fee. Many times, they would beg for a bottle of warm water from our vast supplies. Occasionally, we would give them a piece of candy from our

MREs.Like a seagull lucky enough to swipe a hotdog from a beachgoer's hand, the child receiving a packet of M&Ms or a pre-packaged brownie would flee with their treat as other children chased after them, hoping for a taste.

Inside our makeshift camp, we were soon moved to a new location based on our respective missions. Our new semi-permanent homes consisted of large "temper tents," which were blessed with air conditioning. To this day, I still wonder why the man who invented air conditioning has not been awarded a federal holiday in his honor. To me, it is an invention worthy of a day of gift-giving and feasting, or at least a line of Hallmark greeting cards.

As some days reached highs of 130 degrees or more, proper hydration became critical. Attempts were made to combat the heat by conducting PT at 5:00 a.m. before the world around us became too stifling. However, the heat always won out. A friend of mine from Bravo Company passed out from heat stroke one day. When I inquired about his status with the medics who treated him, I was told that he "had fried the left side of his brain." While I am not sure that this was his official diagnosis, the medics said that when they found him, he kept repeating, "Da, da, da F#$%... Da, da, da F#$%." He was then flown back to Incirlik Air Base for treatment. I never learned what happened to him.

Once settled in our new digs, allied ground combat forces began running patrols into Iraq to assist with the extraction and protection of fleeing Kurdish refugees. Again, my guilt became overwhelming as this mission began. As an infantryman, this is what I should be doing. This is what I had signed up for. Instead, I reported to the Ammo Supply Point (ASP) each morning to conduct my assigned duties. Despite sounding official, the ASP was simply a huge hole in the ground selected to store the unit's ammunition. Day after day, I worked with multiple non-commissioned officers as we organized, counted, secured, and bundled ammunition for transport. One day was spent trying to jerry-rig a netting system to shade the artillery rounds, which were so bombarded by the sun that the protective wax covering their casings was beginning to melt into a thick soup. I don't know if an artillery round can explode because of heat, but it was not an experiment we were willing to engage in.

Like everything else, there were times when we were incredibly busy and times when there was nothing to do. I worked hard and received compliments from many of my superiors. One even went so far as to say, "Even though you're a grunt, you're an excellent Ammunition Specialist." I was very touched by that compliment. It reinforced for me that while I neither wanted nor chose my new specialty, I was doing well at it.

I was also fortunate that working outside in the extreme heat didn't bother me. Maybe my body is inherently good at tolerating heat, or maybe I was just glad to be out of the frigid climate of Germany. Still, it was amazing how cold it felt when the temperature dropped to 85 degrees at night after working in 125-degree heat all day.

The living arrangements in our new tents also proved to be a gift. Our large tent was split into two sections by a pair of large, yet crudely made, wooden shelving units. Our side housed four sergeants, myself, and our lieutenant. The other half was comprised of a half dozen artillerymen, a sergeant, and their captain. I became very close with the artillery guys. What is more surprising is that I became equally close with the Lieutenant and the Captain. It was an unusual arrangement to be so close to, and spend so much time with, officers while being an enlisted man. Evenings were spent hanging out and playing spades, a card game in which two players pair up against two others. On multiple occasions, an artillery friend and I beat the Lieutenant and Captain. This delighted me to no end, and I would begin chanting, "We beat the officers! We beat the officers!" This drew laughter from the others and usually ended in various punishments from the superiors whom I was now mocking. Many times, I was ordered to do push-ups. However, instead of counting, "1... 2... 3..." to mark my push-up progress, I would state in a loud, clear voice, "We... beat... the officers..." On one occasion, after a massive win, I was ordered to take the garbage out.

"Yes, sir," I replied. After collecting the garbage and heading toward the exit, I looked back at the Lieutenant and asked, "Sir? Am I taking the trash out because... We beat the officers? We beat the officers!"

Hearing my mantra yet again, he chased me toward the door as I quickly made my exit.

After another win and my victory cheer, the Captain, who was built like a bodybuilder, simply grabbed me in a bear hug and began wrapping me in duct tape. In many ways, these two men reminded me of my older brother. And like my brother, they dished it out as good as they got it. Really, the only time one of them was actually angry was when we created a makeshift baseball diamond and played a softball tournament. I decided to play with the artillery guys, but since I didn't have a baseball glove, I had to borrow the Lieutenant's. As we took the field each inning, we would pass the glove back and forth. After I robbed the Lieutenant of a hit in the last inning to win 11-7, he said with a noticeable degree of anger, "Gimme my glove," and snatched it from my hand. As he stormed off the field, I quickly surmised that my mantra would not be so casually welcomed this time. As a result, and in a rare turn of events, I strategically decided to remain quiet. Still, both the Lieutenant and I shared one common point of knowledge at that moment...

"We beat the officers! We beat the officers!"

***

As we made our way around our encampment each day, it was not uncommon to come into contact with soldiers from the other countries that made up the coalition. This always made for fun and interesting conversations. One thing that became immediately apparent was that soldiers are the same all over the world. They all tend to excel in two key areas: complaining and busting the chops of the other men they serve with. My daily duties at the Ammo Supply Point brought me into fairly routine contact with a soldier from the Italian army, who must have shared a military specialty similar to mine. I could never actually confirm that because we really had no in-depth way to communicate. He did not speak English, and I did not speak Italian. However, we both spoke a minuscule amount of German that allowed us to share basic information. I learned that his name was Pietro. It was comical to try to discuss our homes and backgrounds based on the language barrier. This typically led to one of us talking while the other simply smiled and nodded in complete befuddlement. Eventually, we landed on one shared love... Star Wars.

With my penchant for imitations, I took deep, raspy breaths and spoke in my closest approximation of James Earl Jones, stating, "Luke, I am your father." Upon hearing my imitation of Darth Vader, Pietro exploded with excitement. Speaking in animated Italian, he expressed how he too loved the Star Wars movies. From that point forward, every time I saw him around the compound, he would wave, dip his chin toward his chest, and begin his own imitation. His Vader-like breathing was passable, but his attempt at a baritone voice was lacking. Still, he would mumble, "Luke, Ima your fatha," and we would both burst out laughing. This same exchange even took place when I saw Pietro standing in line with his fellow Italian soldiers, waiting to enter the chow tent. Upon seeing me, he waved and shot me his Vader imitation. He then pointed me out to his buddies, and they too waved. I can only imagine that he had disclosed to his friends at some point that he met an American troop who talks like Darth Vader. The thought made me smile. That was the time I realized that rapport with another person can be built around the smallest kernel of shared experience. Little did I know that in that same chow hall tent, my strongest bond in that boiling and dusty environment was about to begin.

8

HER

Each day, my tentmates and I would make our way to the chow tent for meals. This required a walk across the camp to a large tan tent and waiting in line behind as many as a hundred other soldiers as they made their way into the air-conditioned makeshift dining hall. The ability to feed so many soldiers three times a day in such a relatively quick fashion was an amazing accomplishment in and of itself. Filling our plates with whatever was being offered that day, we'd carry our trays to one of the many picnic tables lining both sides of the tent's interior. Consistent with the rest of my Army experience, the food was good—not worthy of a gourmet rating, mind you, but certainly acceptable to my non-refined palate.

On one particular day, approximately three weeks after we arrived in Silopi, the chow hall was extremely crowded. My friends and I sat shoulder to shoulder to eat. We tended to remove our head covers while eating, with most guys simply cramming their hats into their side cargo pockets. Perhaps it was my years of playing baseball, but I was a bit more finicky with my hat. The hats we wore were like square baseball caps, very similar to the unique style of baseball hats worn by the Pittsburgh Pirates back in the 1970s and 1980s. I did not like messing up either the brim of my hat or the slight roll I had pinched along the top seam. Moreover, the hours of sweating into my hat and then having it dry out overnight caused it to form perfectly to my head. I did not want to mess with perfection. Ordinarily, had space permitted, I would have set my hat on the bench alongside me. But with no room to do so that day, I placed it under the bench at my feet.

As we sat and ate, I began to hear a very faint squeal—almost like the high-pitched beep you would listen for during a hearing test. Over and over again, the noise persisted.

"Do you guys hear that?" I asked the table. Nobody else seemed to take notice as they gobbled down the day's lunch offerings. Unable to take it anymore, I began to look around for the source of the faint chirp. Then, looking down at my feet, I saw something in my hat. At first, my brain did not quite compute what my eyes were taking in. As I looked closer, I saw a tiny, black furry mass coiled up inside my head covering. When I bent over for a closer peek, a tiny pink nose emerged from the furry clump, and a little mouth full of tiny white teeth opened wide with a squeak.

"Guys, there's a cat in my hat," I said.

The Dr. Seuss homage I unintentionally delivered was not lost on me as I picked up my hat and cradled the little furry creature inside. We all peered down at her as if an extraterrestrial had just landed in the middle of our lunch table. Her little face looked back at the gaggle of giants now staring at her.

"Let's take her back to the tent and keep her as a pet," one of the guys recommended.

Admittedly, this was not an immediate thought of mine. I did not grow up in a pet family, primarily due to my mother. For starters, with a mother who was fastidious about housekeeping and battled obsessive-compulsive tendencies, adding creatures that could disrupt that order was not an option. Equally important was the fact that she did not have a glowing track record with the minor pets permitted in our home.

Years earlier, when my older brother was just a little boy, he had somehow managed to acquire a hamster with whom he could share his love and affection. One winter, while he was at school and my mother was in a flurry of cleaning, she placed the hamster in its cage in the unheated addition attached to the back of our house. What was intended to be just a few moments while she mopped the kitchen floor turned into a disaster as her fevered cleaning pushed the hamster's precarious situation to the back of her mind. Hours later, as her daily cleaning was winding down, she realized she had forgotten to bring the little guy back into the warmth. In a panic, she retrieved the cage, only to find the hamster flat on its back with little frozen legs extended in the air like an upended wooden coffee table. Ignoring basic human logic and not being a zoologist, she brought the cage back inside and placed it next to the radiator, hoping the poor hamster just needed to thaw out before returning to its normal lively self. Even more ridiculously, she silently hoped this miraculous reanimation would occur before my brother returned home from school in an hour or so. The funeral was well-attended.

Her next experience with pets occurred when I was in elementary school. As the school year was winding down and my sister was driving me to school, she hit an unexpected bump in the road. Exiting the vehicle to see what she had run over, we found a box turtle in the middle of the street—a highly unexpected find in Norristown. Somehow, the sturdy reptile survived the encounter with my sister's Monte Carlo. At my insistence, we quickly took the turtle home and placed it in a box. Thanks to this surprise confluence of events, I had found a pet to love.

For weeks, I played with and took care of the turtle, feeding it chunks of tomatoes and lettuce. My father recommended that we drill a hole in the lip of the turtle's shell. According to him, he used to do this with turtles he had found on his dad's small farm when he was a boy. He would then tie a string through the hole and lasso the turtle to the family's clothesline so that it could exercise without wandering off. I not only refused the rudimentary operation, but I also began to understand why we, as a family, were not pet owners.

One day during summer break, while playing with the turtle in the backyard, neighborhood kids called from the alley and asked if I could play. As I made my way out of the yard, I asked my mom to keep an eye on the turtle while she sat on a lounge chair, trying to catch some Vitamin D. Having raised five children, I felt comfortable leaving her in charge of one of the world's slowest-moving creatures. It turned out my confidence in her was grossly misplaced.

Upon returning home, I found my mother dozing in the sun, and the turtle was nowhere to be seen.

"Mom, where's the turtle?" I asked.

Coming to, she looked around our small yard. "It was right here," she said, glancing about, apparently perplexed by the evasive abilities of such a speedy animal.

As mentioned earlier, our backyard was roughly the size of two small bedrooms, bordered by a row of hedges on each side. The turtle was not in the yard; that much was clear. I then began searching the hedges to see if the reptilian Houdini had somehow gotten caught inside. No luck.

To this day, my mother's ability to allow a turtle to escape remains a family legend. Who, after all, can lose a turtle? Fortunately, my mourning over the loss of my beloved hard-shelled friend lasted only a relatively brief period. Nearly two weeks later, a neighbor across the alley found my turtle slowly crawling through his yard. Keep in mind, it took the little creature two weeks to cross the alley, but my mom somehow managed to lose him in about half an hour.

In light of this sad family history, keeping the small kitten that had taken up residence in my hat as a pet did not immediately occur to me. However, everyone at our lunch table liked the idea.

I took the tiny furry blob from my hat and held it to my chest. It continued to chirp at me as I put my hat back on. Before we all left with our newfound prize, I grabbed a couple of uneaten pieces of chicken from one of the guys' plates, and we made for the exit.

***

As we returned to our tent, I placed the little kitten on my bunk. As she walked around my Army blanket and smelled her new surroundings, we all got a better look at her. She was jet black on top with a white belly, paws, and muzzle. The white around her face gave her an air of attentiveness and curiosity. She must have been quite young because she was not much bigger than a coffee mug. Her exploration of my bunk led her to find the perfect spot of comfort, and she plopped down, looking at us as we collectively stared back at her, each trying to figure out the other.

"We should make her a litter box," someone suggested. It was another brilliant idea.

I removed the small serrated folding knife I kept with me, retrieved a box, and cut it down to a small lip. While litter was not readily available, our new world was surrounded by dry, dusty dirt. I then stepped outside, filled the box with some dirt, and placed it next to my bed. Out of curiosity, I picked the little furball up and placed her next to the new handmade litter box. After a few sniffs, she climbed onto the pile of dirt and squatted. In amazement, I watched as she immediately produced a tiny circle of liquid and then covered it up with her back paws. I'm sure any cat owner on the planet would immediately recognize the feline instinct behind the behavior I had just witnessed, but to me, it was nothing less than unadulterated brilliance.

"Oh my God," I said to the other witnesses. "Did you see that? She just went to the bathroom where she was supposed to. That's smarter than at least half of you."

Everyone laughed at my keen, though potentially offensive, observation. I then picked up our new mascot and gently began to pet her.

She seemed to relish the attention.

"What do we name her?" someone asked.

The question hung in the air for only a moment before someone tossed out a deep and heartfelt option: "How about Shithead?"

It's important to remember that we were all soldiers of the United States Army. No one in the tent had been reading

Tolstoy or dozing off to the gentle stylings of Chopin. Except for the captain and lieutenant, no one in the tent had a college education. In light of who we were as a collective, the moniker seemed acceptable. And so, our new little friend became "Shithead."

Figuring she was probably hungry, I held up a tiny piece of leftover chicken in front of her. She immediately scarfed down the morsel and a few more.

"She even likes chow hall chicken," I noted aloud. "She's definitely a keeper." The small crowd that had gathered nodded in agreement.

"Maybe we should give her a bath," someone then blurted out.

Despite the lack of advanced education in the room, brilliant ideas continued to flutter around the interior of the tent. She was cute, tiny, and sweet, but also a tad dusty and stinky.

One of the two staff sergeants who shared our half of the tent had temporarily returned to Berlin on leave, leaving his gear and personal items behind. Among those items was a round 5-gallon Igloo water jug. This particular sergeant was quite fussy about his appearance and fastidious about his gear; the term "anal retentive" would probably be a more fitting description. However, one of the junior sergeants correctly pointed out that since he wasn't here at the moment, what he didn't know wouldn't hurt him. Everyone nodded in agreement, and the missing sergeant's water jug became the prime receptacle for our new addition's first bath. So, with the warm plastic water bottles that seemed to be everywhere in the tent, we filled up the commandeered water jug. Someone used a bar of soap, and with a few rubs of the hand, added a touch of bubbles to our water cooler day spa.

Despite having never owned a cat, I vaguely remembered cartoons from my childhood in which cats seemed to detest water, often comically sprinting away from it in hasty retreat. Still, I did not fully comprehend at that moment that these cartoons were an example of art imitating life. And so, we set about trying to put a cat in a water jug filled with soapy water. Her little paws grabbed for the side of the jug as we attempted to place her into what we all thought was a delightful little bubble bath. I would remove one hooked claw only to have the other three attach. I would then attempt to remove those claws only to have the first paw cling to safety again. Our new cat suddenly felt like an octopus as I tried to convince her of the value of a much-needed tub.

After some gentle cajoling, the little black bundle was lowered neck-deep into a lukewarm bath. With a few quick chirps of disagreement, our new friend succumbed to a necessary scrubbing. After her bath, I took her out and dried her off. Already, she looked more presentable—at least until my sergeant assistant noted several black specks on her white belly. A handful of tiny gnats had apparently made a home in the soft white fur on her undercarriage. "I'll get some tweezers," Sarge announced.

Then, as I held her down, Sarge delicately plucked the prickly intruders from her fur. Our once-dusty visitor had suddenly become a cleaned and coiffed mascot worthy of any desert-rated cat show. I returned her to my bunk, where she took it upon herself to finish the bath we had started before finally conking out for an afternoon nap. As she slept,

I made a mental note to never drink anything out of that particular Igloo water jug again.

***

That evening, in addition to hanging out and playing cards, the kitten was passed around the tent and petted by those who were interested. Luckily, neither the Captain nor the Lieutenant had a problem with our feline acquisition. However, lights out posed a problem. What was I going to do with her? I didn't want to roll over on her in the middle of the night if she stayed on my bunk, and I didn't want her to run away like a particular turtle I once owned. So, I placed a blanket at the bottom of a tall box and put her inside, where she quickly curled up and seemed to settle down. Placing the box next to my bunk, I fell asleep, confident in the depths of my parenting genius.

Not unlike a human newborn that refuses to sleep through the night, the quiet we all experienced at lights out was short-lived. A couple of hours later, the kitten found her voice. With much louder screeches than the ones she had introduced me to at our initial meeting in the chow tent that day, Shithead belted out an unrequested song of displeasure for all of my tentmates to hear. She was clearly not pleased at being confined in a box.

Despite being awakened in such an unpleasant manner, the Lieutenant offered me a surprisingly tender range of options to choose from. "Beyer, get that freakin' cat out of here, or I'm going to step on its head."

I guess the option was not really much of an option after all. Groggily, I reached next to my bed and gently tipped the box over on its side so the tiny, shrieking songstress could be freed from her loving cardboard prison. Sadly, I watched as she skittered from the box and ran from the tent.

'Well, it was fun while it lasted,' I thought to myself as I turned back over to go to sleep, feeling more than a little sad over our failed mascot experiment.

The next morning, however, I was awakened by an odd and unexpected alarm clock. As I lay in my bunk, I could feel something tickling my hair. Thinking one of the guys must be messing with me, I reached up to flick their hand away. Surprisingly, my movement was met not with the grubby hand of a morning jokester, but with a handful of soft fur. The tickling I felt was actually the kitten licking the top of my head. The late-night fugitive had not only returned, but she sought me out for the second time in as many days. The motivation for the licking was open for debate. Maybe it was an apology for causing a ruckus the previous evening. Maybe it was her little sign of affection. Or maybe I had made it through the first twenty years of life without knowing that I tasted delicious.

Regardless of the reason, one thing became crystal clear: she now belonged to me.

9

TIME FLIES

To be quite honest, the most enjoyable time I spent in the military was during the deployment to Silopi, Turkey. Living out of tents, working in 120-degree heat, and taking ice-cold portable showers that frequently backed up, leaving you standing ankle-deep in the previous guy's shower water, does not make for an enticing holiday getaway advertisement. In actuality, it was the camaraderie that made this time enjoyable. Growing up, I had always noticed how large snowfalls seemed to bring people together. Neighbors would be forced outside to shovel parking spaces in front of their homes. They would stop and chat as they shoveled up to where one homeowner's piece of sidewalk ended and the next neighbor's began. Pairings of neighbors that seemed unlikely to occur in sunny weather came together on these snowy days to shovel the walks and parking spaces of older residents. Not only did these large snow coverings make the world seem cleaner and cozier, but in the wake of these snowfalls, everyone in southeastern Pennsylvania shared one unified undertaking: to dig out from what Mother Nature had dropped on us. Neighbors discussed the weather as they worked together. Fathers who would have been at work at this time of day were home with their families. Older siblings who typically had no time for their younger siblings were suddenly caught in the act of building a snow fort, sledding, or hurling a snowball at a fleeing and giggling neighbor child. The circumstances and shared workload that came with large snowfalls always seemed to bring people together, if only for a brief period of time.

It felt very much the same way during those months in Turkey. The heat, the dirt, the mission—it brought us all together without distraction. The simplicity of the whole experience made it a time of togetherness. Now, with the addition of our new friend, an even greater sense of levity existed in our tent.

The cardboard cage was no longer an option, and thanks to her unexpected return, it was obvious that she wanted to be with us, or more specifically, with me. She was now free to roam around as she pleased, but rarely did she go outside. Like a rebellious teenager, being told she couldn't go out only made her want to go out more. However, after her late-night escape, she must have realized just how well she had it in the clean, air-conditioned tent. Her departure and return made me wonder if she felt the need to tell her family that she was moving in with a new one.

I have no idea where she slept before she found me, but now she spent her days dozing in and out of sleep on my bunk in delightful air conditioning. Food was hand-delivered to her as I brought her treats from the chow tent. Pieces of chicken and little scoops of tuna were polished off quickly and efficiently. She simply became one of the guys. Some people ignored her; others fussed over her like little old ladies, but she was always in the mix. At night, she slept with me. Tending to sleep on my stomach, she would rest on top of my poncho liner, which I used as a blanket. Any concerns about rolling on top of her in the middle of the night quickly disappeared as she learned to ride the wave of the blanket like a championship surfer as I changed positions. Whenever I moved, she would wait for me to settle before returning to her resting spot with a soft plop. On one particular evening, it must have felt colder than usual because she woke me up batting at the blanket near my face. Tap, tap, tap. Over and over again.

"What?" I asked her in the darkness. As she continued to bat at me, I lifted the blanket a few inches in an attempt to understand. It was exactly what she wanted because she immediately crawled under the blanket and back between my legs. She had made her point perfectly clear: 'Hey, I'm cold. Let me get under the blanket.'

And just like that, I learned to speak cat... or Turkish... or Turkish cat.

This routine occurred frequently as the heat of August began to fade into the slightly cooler weather of September. In anticipation of the rainy weather likely to occur in the fall, we decided to build wooden floors in our large tent to counteract the inordinate amounts of mud that wet weather would surely bring. The construction meant moving our bunks and belongings around the tent. For her own protection, we placed her on the top shelf of one of the wooden bookcases that separated our portion of the tent from the artillery guys. Without an apparent care in the world, she curled up on the shelf and kept a watchful gaze on our progress in between her cat naps.

This little kitten must have known which side of her bread was buttered because she excelled in simply going with the flow. She rarely meowed. She never caused a problem. She just went along to get along.

As I moved around the compound, it appeared that I was not the only individual who had found a pet. Wild dogs had also found their way into the camp. They, like our little kitten, were quickly domesticated as a result of regular meals and attention. It was not uncommon to see a dog sitting in front of a tent, watching the world go by. In many ways, the whole situation took on the feeling of how man's relationship with his animals must have developed as civilizations were being created.

Unfortunately, someone in a position of authority had reached a breaking point with these so-called pets. Word went out that all animals in camp were to be collected and put down. The official reason given was to prevent the spread of rabies. A tent-to-tent search was conducted by the Military Police to collect the stray animals that had found a home among the soldiers. It was decided in our tent that we would hide our little friend like a feline Anne Frank. I quickly dumped out the makeshift litter box and secreted the cat into a Humvee. I then drove to the Ammo Supply Point and waited for word that the grand animal round-up had been completed. Upon receiving word that the coast was clear, I returned to the tent. No one was ever the wiser, and our secret remained hidden among our small group.

***

Our time in Turkey began to move quickly as the weeks rattled by in fast succession. The only wrinkle occurred when we were made aware of a possible attack on our camp. Being ten years before 9/11, terrorism was not a word that was often thrown around at that time. However, it had come to our leadership's attention that the anniversary of some historical attack was approaching. The concern was that some individuals from an unspecified group might attempt to access the Ammo Supply Point to obtain the munitions necessary to attack U.S. and allied forces. It therefore became necessary for our unit to protect the Ammo Supply Point if an attack was initiated.

Thankfully, the U.S. Army Ranger tab on our Lieutenant's shoulder indicated that he had completed Ranger training at some point in his career. Unfortunately, he was the only other person in our unit, besides myself, who was trained in infantry tactics. Again, I had been reassigned to a unit of truck drivers.

In anticipation of a possible attack, the Lieutenant took our group to the Ammo Supply Point, where we laid out our thoughts on where the attack might be launched from, what our positions would be, and how we would defend the critical contents of this piece of land. This type of planning was not new to me, but for a group of truck drivers, the Lieutenant seemed to be speaking a different language. As we discussed the specifics, I began to feel worried about the capabilities of my fellow soldiers. They were good guys, but they knew as much about this type of thing as I had known about driving a stick shift when I first joined the unit. If this went down, it would be like playing a baseball game with a team full of drama club members. While there is obviously nothing wrong with people who enjoy the thrill of acting, there is no reason to believe that those skills will easily translate to hitting a fastball or turning a double play. The same rationale held true for the others in my unit. This realization brought me a great deal of concern.

On the specified anniversary date a couple of days later, we all tried to go about our business, but there was a distinct air of distraction that seemed to engulf us. It was explained to us that if the attack were going to happen, it would most likely occur that evening. We readied our gear and weapons as we waited for the call. Standing in front of the tent, I chatted with one of the guys in our unit. He was a husband, a father, and a man trained by the U.S. Army to drive tractor trailers. He seemed distracted as we talked, and I certainly knew why. This was the first time in my life that I had to wonder if I would exist twenty-four hours from now.

We have all heard stories of people who were alive one day and dead the next: victims of freak accidents, victims of drunk drivers, victims of unforeseen widow-maker heart attacks. The difference between this situation and those people was the Catch-22 brought about by knowing something was headed your way. Those people didn't know what was coming for them. If they did, would they have done something differently in their last few hours of life? Should we be doing something differently now? What I was feeling was not actually fear; it was more of a crude amalgamation of curiosity, a desire for preparation, and the impetuousness of youth. Will I be here tomorrow? Is there anything I could be doing to help ensure that I will be? If you are going to attack us, can we just get it started already? I'm guessing that this same self-talk was going on in the mind of my colleague. Sadly, all we could do for the time being was wait. So, as always, I talked to God, asked Him for His protection, and listened for the call.

Thankfully, the call never came. There was no attack, and the anniversary date came and went without incident. The sunrise the following morning brought with it a sense of relief. I am not sure why our superiors thought that if an attack were to come, it would only be on the anniversary date. However, if they weren't worried, then neither was I.

That evening, while lying on my stomach on my bunk, I wrote a letter home to my parents with a kitten curled up on my butt. I did not tell my parents about what could have happened the previous evening. There was no sense in worrying them. Instead, I asked my father for some help. I inquired if he could start obtaining applications for universities in the Philadelphia area. I was only a few months away from completing my term of service with the Army, and it was time to start thinking about my future and what I wanted to do with the rest of my life.

Strangely enough, after my experiences at Fort Benning, the Berlin Brigade, and Turkey, college no longer seemed so scary to me.

10

THE GREAT ESCAPE

F or three months, my days vacillated between incredibly busy and totally boring. When men get bored, games invariably get created to kill the time. A sergeant friend and I invented a home run derby game in which we used a wooden axe handle to hit rocks at the Ammo Supply Point. We would toss a rock into the air, and if it traveled at least a predetermined distance after being hit, it was considered a home run. Each home run earned a point, and it actually became a pastime that we looked forward to. For morning PT, we would sometimes play soccer in the early hours before the heat of the day set in. It was not uncommon for a volleyball tournament to break out. On Labor Day, we celebrated with a unit-wide cookout. Burgers and hot dogs were grilled, and much to the pleasure of many of my fellow soldiers, each troop was granted two beers. Not being a drinker, I passed mine along to one of my artillery buddies who grew up minutes from me in Phoenixville, Pennsylvania. I was more than happy to share my drinks with a fellow Eagles fan. As for the Cowboys fan who also lived in our tent... well, he could go drink a nice tall glass of toilet water for all I cared. The bond between soldiers can only be stretched so thin.

Since there had been no alcohol in camp up to that point, the promise of an ice-cold beer whipped many of the troops into a frenzy. To monitor alcohol intake, soldiers had their hands stamped once they received their two beers. In typical government fashion, the cheapest ink was used for this purpose. Many of the troops soon discovered that they could easily wash the ink off in the bathroom and jump back into line for additional drinks. As a result, a considerable number of soldiers were feeling no pain that day. It was a good day for many.

On an unrelated evening, several soldiers succumbed to a disastrous mix of boredom and poor judgment. They stole some ammunition and took their weapons into downtown Silopi. I have no idea what their ultimate plans were, but after causing some vandalism, the Military Police caught them. These must have been additional troops who had parts of their brains fried by the heat. Since we, as soldiers, represented the United States of America in this distant sandy corner of the world, I quietly hoped that these idiots would face severe consequences for their actions. This type of idiocy made all of us look bad.

Throughout my time in Turkey, there were two things I looked forward to: attending the available church service on Sundays and returning to my tent each night to see my little feline friend. The feeling must have been mutual because when I returned to my bunk each day, she would immediately stand at her own form of attention in hopes of a back scratch. In the dirt and stench that permeated a world where everyone you interacted with was not only a man but also a U.S. soldier, I found comfort in her presence. As an Army soldier, it was a welcome break to have a little piece of sweetness in my life. Still, on some level, she must have liked the stench of this world, because whenever I tossed my uniform top on the bunk, she would invariably find the sweatiest part and roll around in it. I'm not saying she was bright, but she seemed to love me... or at least she loved that smell.

***

At that time, there were two clocks in my life counting down simultaneously. One was the end of the Turkey deployment. The second, the grander of the two clocks, was counting down my term of service in the military. December 10, 1991, which had once seemed eons away, had dropped from a three-digit countdown to a two-digit countdown as my days in Turkey ticked by. The light was now at the end of the tunnel, and shockingly, the estimate for our involvement in Operation Provide Comfort II proved to be accurate. At the three-month point, our time was up.

This news that our unit would be returning to Berlin in mid-October not only brought excitement to each of us, but for me, it also presented an interesting dilemma.

"What are you going to do with the cat?" one of the guys pulled me aside and asked.

Up to this point, I hadn't really thought about the endpoint of this relationship.

As if sensing my inner turmoil, he shared a much-needed dose of reality. "You can't leave her here. You've been feeding her and taking care of her for months," he pointed out. Everything he said was true. I certainly couldn't leave her behind. But the next part was going to be tricky. After all, the cat was not military property. Moreover, a sweep had already been conducted by the MPs to collect all the animals and exterminate them. How do I explain this new addition to my property sheet? Would I have to admit to deliberately violating orders by hiding an animal? Do I lie and say that I found the cat after the round-up? Would they even let me take the cat on the plane? All of these questions swirled through my head as we began packing our gear in preparation for our departure.

Like our arrival, our departure would require a 14-hour bus ride across southern Turkey. This would be the first leg I needed to figure out. As we continued to pack, more of my tentmates realized that Shithead would have to come with us. This raised communal questions about what to do. Then, from the very same group of geniuses who devised a plan to give a dusty little kitten a bath in a missing colleague's water jug, a soldier stepped forward with an old duffle bag. "We could just stick her in a duffle bag, and no one would know." Yet again, pure genius.

So, on the date of our departure, I boarded the bus with a cat in a sack. I took a seat near one of the windows as my tentmates took seats around me to buffer my hidden cargo from other soldiers unaware of our plan. The tiny creature must have somehow known that she was now the basis of a secret mission because she did not make a sound as I carried her around in the bag. Once the bus started rolling, I removed her from the duffle bag and placed her on my lap. There she sat for hour after hour as I stroked her back, both of us fading in and out of sleep. She never made a noise. More surprisingly, she never went to the bathroom. She just sat contentedly in my lap and waited for what was to come next.

Upon returning to Incirlik Air Base, I placed her back in the duffle bag as we exited the bus. Unlike the C5 Galaxy we flew in on, the return trip would be much more comfortable. The flight, provided by the Military Airlift Command of the U.S. Air Force, resembled a commercial aircraft. As we waited at the airbase for our flight, I sneaked over to a patch of grass, took the kitten from the bag, and placed her on the ground. As if sensing my intention, she quickly peed in the grass and attempted to cover what she left behind with her paws. Then back in the bag she went.

We were informed that our rucksacks and duffle bags would be checked and stored under the plane. This set off alarm bells in my head. As the military bags were collected for transfer onto the plane, I realized that a change needed to be made. I obviously could not leave her in a pile with the rest of the gear, nor were we allowed to take personal bags onto the flight. I would have to find a way to keep her with me. The question was: how could this be accomplished?

Then it occurred to me. To carry our ammunition magazines, canteen, and related gear, we wore what the Army referred to as a Load Bearing Equipment (LBE) harness, which consisted of a web belt and suspenders. Attached to this belt and hanging against our upper thigh was our gas mask, kept in an 8" x 10" canvas bag. For context, the bag was slightly smaller than a sheet of notebook paper and slightly wider than a soup can. To access the mask, you unsnapped the fold-over flap that faced the front of your body. Unless I decided to fold the poor cat in half and stick her in my pocket, this was the only other available option.

I explained my plan to a couple of the guys standing in front of me to provide cover from any onlookers. I then removed my gas mask and stuffed it inside my already crammed rucksack. With the gas mask carrier now empty, I took our little friend from the duffle bag and placed her inside the gas mask carrier. Again, as if understanding my dilemma, she did not resist the relocation and allowed herself to be placed in the tight quarters. Crisis averted. Now all we had to do was wait for our flight.

Word must have spread to our other tentmates because, as we stood in the hangar, various soldiers approached me at different times, leaning in with a conspiratorial tone.

"How's our girl doing?" they would ask.

"So far, so good," I would reply.

In typical military fashion, the wait seemed interminable. To check on her, I would stick my finger in the tiny opening created by the fold-over flap. When I did, my finger would be greeted with a tiny lick as if to say, "I'm here. We're all good." Like a dolphin cresting the surface of the water for a breath of air, her tiny pink nose would occasionally poke through the same opening, looking for some fresh air of her own. I would then rub her nose with my finger as if to say, "I'm here. We're all good."

The whole process was a miserable experience. As an inherent rule follower employed by an organization that demanded adherence to all rules, what I was doing caused me a great deal of anxiety. I felt like I was teetering on an ethical balance beam over a pit filled with jagged rocks of consequences. However, each time her little pink nose appeared from the carrier, I felt a surge of justification in what I was trying to do.

***

After a couple of hours of waiting, it was finally time to board the flight. We were home free, or so I thought. Word suddenly came down from our superior officers that officials from the Turkish government would have to inspect our weapons and review the serial numbers before we boarded the flight. I assumed this was done to ensure that we weren't smuggling weapons out of their country or something, but who knows? All I knew for certain was that I would have to stand face-to-face with a Turkish official, hoping that the cat hiding in the small bag on my hip would not meow. Panic made a dramatic reappearance as some of my tentmates shot me worried glances.

So, we lined up to board the massive jet. As I stood there waiting my turn, the movie "Midnight Express" played on an incessant loop in my brain. At that point in my life, I wasn't even sure that I had seen the movie. But I was quite certain it was a true story about a young man who had been sent to a Turkish prison for trying to smuggle drugs out of Turkey.

"Oh my God," I thought to myself. "Am I about to take a starring role in an international incident?"

Tiny rivers of sweat began to trickle down my lower back and pool in the waistband of my uniform pants. Soldier after soldier approached the Turkish officials, showed them their M-16s, and waited for the signal to board. As I approached the front of the line, a little pink nose popped up in the gap of the carrier, but this time she made a tiny meow. I would like to think she was wishing me good luck, but my panic did not allow for such thoughts at that moment. Instead, I took my helmet and covered the hole and as much of the carrier as possible, hoping that if another meow was forthcoming, the Kevlar helmet would help to muffle the sound.

Not knowing the exact reason for the inspection, a thought suddenly occurred to me: what if they asked to see our gas masks? My already pounding heartbeat began to feel like a jackhammer in my chest.

"Dear God, please be with me. Please help me get through this."

Finally, it was my turn to approach the Turkish officials.

"Be cool. Just relax," I said to myself, hoping some self-talk would help mask the unbridled terror I was feeling.

I handed my rifle over just as the others before me had done. The process felt like walking through a magnetometer at the airport. Despite not having any weapons on you, you still tend to flinch as you walk through, listening for an alarm to go off. As much as I tried to appear normal, I felt like I was engaged in a full-body flinch that would give away what I was doing.

The officials looked at the weapon I handed them, noted the serial number, and then motioned for me to board the plane.

I made it. I was through. I fought back both tears and vomit as the gas pedal of my sympathetic nervous system was suddenly replaced by the harsh braking of my parasympathetic nervous system. While my knees felt weak as I climbed the steps to the gangway, my heart rate slowly began to return to normal. Entering the plane, the air conditioning felt like the comfort of a rich ocean breeze. I was one step closer to home, or at least Berlin.

I then made my way to the back of the aircraft, following the soldiers in line ahead of me. As I approached, I saw the faces of the men with whom I had spent nearly every minute of the last three months. They appeared to share my fear over what I had just gone through, as they all looked at me intently with wide eyes. Their faces resembled those of an expectant father in a waiting room, anxiously anticipating word from the doctor. Collectively, their expressions seemed to ask a one-word question: "Well?"

I nodded and gave a thumbs-up, letting them know that our little stowaway was still with us. In unison, they cheered, causing others in the unit, who were unaware of our secret mission, to look back at the source of the commotion. Their excitement over our arrival on the plane touched me. But what was even more moving was their seat selection. This was not a commercial flight with assigned seating; we simply filled up the available seats. What I saw was a sea of friendly faces with one open seat directly in the middle.

The message was clear: "We saved this seat for you, and we'll help shield your little girl from the flight attendants."

I smiled as I took my seat, surrounded by friends. The pats on my back as I sat down said it all: We made it. We all made it.

11

THE BOYS (AND GIRL) ARE BACK IN TOWN

T he return to Berlin in mid-October 1991 was much more enjoyable than my initial arrival in January 1990. Regardless of the enjoyment I experienced during our deployment to Turkey, I was still glad to be home. Home—a concept that has definitely changed throughout my lifetime. As a child, I had one home. It was where my parents and siblings lived. It was where my bedroom and toys were. It was where my mom washed my clothes, made our dinners, and packed our lunches for school. It was where you returned after the school day ended or upon completing our baseball and football games. The concept of home was very clear then. But as I progressed through my time in the military, "home" took on a more simplistic meaning. Once you start navigating the world around you and moving from place to place, you learn that home is where your stuff is. For me, my stuff was in a room at the McNair Barracks in Berlin, and it felt good to return to the things I had taken for granted: an actual bed with sheets, a consistently hot shower, television, movies, music, and of course, my friends who did not participate in the deployment. I looked forward to seeing all of these things again.

Once we landed, my poor feline traveling companion was forced back into her tiny confines. For a good portion of the trip, I had been able to keep her on my lap, hidden from the military flight attendants. When we were served food on the flight, she went back into the gas mask carrier. We were too close to home now to raise questions from a flight attendant. Realizing she must be starving, I shared my meal with her. Taking pinches of food from my plate, I slipped it through the gap between the folding flap and the base of the carrier. The same opening that allowed her to take tiny gasps of fresh air during our trip also enabled her to eat. She already seemed aware of the food, as her tiny pink nose poked through the hole, sniffing at what must have been an intoxicating aroma. I could feel her lapping at the little pinches of food hungrily as I placed them inside the small opening of the carrier. Her ability to hold it together throughout the entire unorthodox travel process left me in awe of the little blob of fur.

Boarding the buses at the airport to return to the barracks, I could feel the excitement among the group. While many of our unit members were single guys, we also had a fair share of married men and dads. If I was excited to get back to my barracks room, I can only imagine how it felt to return to a wife and children.

As the bus pulled into the barracks through the front gate and drove toward 6th Battalion Headquarters, I saw something I had never seen before at this location: a crowd. A sizable group of people gathered outside the 6th Battalion area, waving to us as we approached. Wives and kids clapped and cheered, hoping to catch a glimpse of their returning soldier. Some wives cried, and some children hopped up and down with excitement as if they were waiting their turn to sit on Santa's lap. It was very much a Norman Rockwell scene, and you couldn't help but get caught up in the excitement of the impending reunification of loved ones.

Despite the joy and commotion, I felt very alone at that moment. There were no loved ones waiting for me—no wife or girlfriend to hug, no children to cling to my pant legs. I had made the mistake of finding a girlfriend the summer before joining the Army, but I received the 'Dear John' phone call more than six months ago. Apparently, the distance had become too much of an issue. Now, I was forced to live vicariously through those guys returning to their families. I was excited for them, but that did not compensate for the loneliness I felt at the time.

As soldiers began exiting the bus, they entered the crowd, which was bouncing around like numbered ping pong balls waiting to be selected for the Power Ball drawing. The unbridled happiness of families coming together after months of separation lifted my own mood as I made my way toward the bus door. Holding my little armful of black fur like a football, I exited the bus and felt the cool fall air of Berlin. It was a welcome change from where we had been since the summer.

It was also time for goodbyes. We shook hands with one another and wished each other luck. For those of us in the same platoon, we would obviously see each other again at work in a few days. For those from different platoons, we would likely catch one another at the chow hall or the Post Exchange. But in either case, it would be different.

Every year, high school football players say goodbye to their teammates after their final game of the senior season. Despite the fact that they will all see each other the next day at school, the sense of loss accompanying these farewells can be profound. After four years of sweating, bleeding, and fighting with their teammates to conquer the gridiron yard by yard under the lights on Friday evenings, senior football players cannot fight the emotions associated with the knowledge that those battles are over. Admittedly and thankfully, our deployment was not a war. We did not lose brothers in a hail of gunfire. Still, we were together all the time—the dirt, the heat, the job, the worries, the food, the jokes—we experienced all of these things together. Then, through the miracle of modern air travel, all that togetherness just ended. We all returned to the lives we knew before. That's what made my return home, or at least my return to my belongings, feel a little sad at that moment.

Luckily for me, my sadness was mitigated by what I was now carrying in my arms. True, I did not have a wife or girlfriend waving a flag, holding a sign for me, or jumping into my arms. True, I did not have kids screaming "Daddy" and trying to knock me off my feet with their exuberance. But what I did have was a new responsibility. I now had to take care of somebody else besides myself. I had a little stowaway who required my love and attention. Much like new parents immediately after the birth of their child, I realized that getting her here was just the beginning.

After the handshakes and pats on the back, I grabbed my duffel bag, rucksack, and helmet and prepared to walk to my barracks room. This proved more difficult than I had initially anticipated while cradling a kitten in my arms. Since she had just traveled non-stop for 19 hours in and out of a sack without complaint, I assumed she was up for one more inconvenience. So, I picked her up and placed her on my right shoulder, not unlike a pirate with his parrot. She took a second to balance herself as I felt her front and back claws dig into the heavy material of my uniform top. Grabbing my duffel bag in one hand and my rucksack and helmet in the other, off we went to my barracks room and her new home. Shifting her weight back and forth to stabilize herself as I walked, she looked around, taking it all in. Her little life had changed drastically once again. If she had concerns about this new and impending aspect of her life, she certainly didn't share them with me.

***

Entering my barracks room, I dropped my gear at the door and removed Shithead from my shoulder.

"You did real good, kid," I said as I held her in front of me.

With a kiss on her head, I placed her on my bed. Her nose went a mile a minute as she sniffed all around and explored her new environment. As she scouted things out, I realized three things needed to happen fairly quickly. First, I needed to get to the PX and buy her a litter box, some litter, and some actual cat food. Second, I needed to research where I could get her a checkup and the shots that I assumed a new cat would need. Lastly, I had to change her name. If I didn't leave her behind in Turkey, I certainly wasn't going to leave her behind in Germany. And if she was coming home with me to Norristown, I couldn't have my parents calling her "Shithead." But first things first—she needed some basic necessities. I quickly changed into civilian clothes and headed for the bus stop. After more than 19 hours of traveling, I was exhausted myself. But such is the life of a parent, and my little girl needed to eat.

When I returned to my barracks room later that day, I quickly filled the new litter box with litter. She immediately jumped down off the bed, perched herself upon the litter, and went and went and went. The poor thing had obviously been holding it in forever. I felt bad for that, but our travel situation was not exactly normal. My appreciation for her flexibility throughout our trek was beyond words. It kept us both out of hot water. Still, I couldn't help but think that somewhere in her little pea brain, she knew what was being asked of her and why.

After what seemed like minutes, she covered up her business, climbed out of the litter box, and made her way to the new plastic bowl I had just purchased. One side was filled with fresh water, and the other with dry cat food. The folks at Purina must know their business because she quickly attacked the crunchy nuggets. After months of chow hall food, she clearly loved something that was more focused on her feline taste buds.

As I watched her eat, it occurred to me: Silopi... I'll call her Silopi. It rolled off the tongue easily, was much more socially appropriate than what we had been calling her, and was a fitting tribute to where our story began.

After a quick drink of water, Silopi climbed back onto the bed and stretched out, her bladder empty and her belly full. Her little black-and-white body curled up on my olive drab army blanket seemed to reflect her very existence in my life. She was tiny, sweet, and not issued to me by the military. She stood out on the blanket and, in many ways, stood out in my life. After two years of worrying about myself and my own lot in life—worrying and complaining—she was a stark reminder that my life should not be so self-focused. She was an unexpected surprise in the desert that helped me realize there was more to life than my own wants and needs. She was God's gentle nudge, telling me to worry about someone besides myself.

After a few minutes of back scratches, her eyes became heavy. Leaving her to doze, I walked to the payphone just outside our building. I needed to tell my parents that I was back in Berlin safely. More importantly, I needed to let them know that in a matter of eight weeks, I'd be returning to Norristown with a little friend. Hopefully, my mom would be okay with it. Given her past experiences with hamsters and turtles, I hoped Silopi would be okay with it, too.

***

After very infrequent phone calls home over the last several months, my parents were glad to hear my voice and relieved to know I had returned to Berlin safely. They were amazed by the tale of my cat rescue, and though somewhat tentative, my mother gave a thumbs-up to Silopi joining the family.

"Well... what's a Turkish cat like?" my mom asked.

I think, on some level, she must have thought I was bringing home some wild bobcat trapped out in the desert. While she was glad I would soon be home from the Army, I'm certain she was picturing a saber-toothed tiger roaming through her living room.

"Mom, she's just a cat," I explained.

"And what's her name?" she asked.

"Silopi. Like 'Sa-Low-Pea,'" I said, sounding it out for her.

Her agreement was far from exuberant, but it was an agreement nonetheless.

The rest of the day was spent reconnecting with my former infantry pals who had transferred with me to the 6th Battalion. They were also fascinated by my story as I introduced them to Silopi. After being surrounded by a tent full of men for the first few months of her life, she warmed to them instantly.

At that time, I had only one other roommate who was in the process of being transferred to another duty station. I didn't know him well, but he was never around. It couldn't have been a better arrangement for Silopi and me. Since pets were obviously not allowed in the barracks, I only had to hide her for two more months. It should be a piece of cake.

That night, as I climbed into an actual bed with freshly laundered sheets, I reflected on my time in Turkey. The whole experience seemed like a whirlwind. Being back in Berlin, I realized just how close I was to being discharged. It was an exciting thought.

Lying in the darkness, I felt Silopi jump onto the bed. She made her way onto my chest and plopped down, inviting me to pet her. I said my prayers as I stroked her back. This was the beginning of our new life together and the eve of my new life beyond the military. I remembered the guy I met when I first came to Berlin who was getting ready to be discharged. He was so happy about returning home to Michigan, and I was so jealous. Now, I found myself in the same position. It seemed like it took twenty-five years to get to this point. At the same time, it felt like it took two weeks. Time is funny that way: the days are long, but the years are short.

I then felt Silopi batting at the blanket near my face. Instinctively, I lifted the covers and felt her slide down between the sheets as she took up her usual position between my legs. Soon, we were both asleep as visions of being discharged from the Army danced in my head.

12

AUF WIEDERSEHEN (GOODBYE)

In the weeks after my return, it seemed like I had CQ Duty an awful lot. This was a particularly miserable assignment that rotated among soldiers within the unit. It required you to sit at a desk outside the First Sergeant's office for a period of twenty-four hours. You answered any incoming calls and completed any menial tasks the front office threw at you. After everyone went home for the day or returned to their barracks rooms for personal time, you stayed on in the event of an emergency. It was long and boring. I am fairly certain that since I would soon be discharged from the Army, I was given this undesirable duty to spare the others. It was a way of passive-aggressively saying, "Screw you since you aren't staying."

When I was still in 4th Battalion, my Platoon Sergeant approached me about taking the Sergeant's test, which would have allowed me to become a non-commissioned officer (NCO). I was honored by this urging since I had been in the Army for less than two years at the time. Truth be told, since I was firmly settled in and the time was rolling by, I had briefly considered re-enlisting. However, the move to 6th Battalion cured me of that thought rather quickly. So, I operated under the belief that my decision to leave the military was being rewarded with routine CQ duty.

The nice thing about CQ duty was that you had the next day off. Generally, this meant sleeping most of the day to make up for the sleep lost during your twenty-four-hour shift. For me, it meant that I could make my way to the medical detachment to get Silopi her veterinary checkup and required shots. To no great surprise, she took both like a champ.

The evening solitude that came with CQ duty was also good for writing letters home to friends and family. It also meant filling out the college applications that my father had been good enough to mail to me. I think he was excited about my interest in college. I would be the first (and ultimately the only) of his five children to attend a four-year university. We had always joked about my father that if one of his children were in Bangkok, Thailand, and needed a pencil, he would be there the following morning with a freshly sharpened Dixon-Ticonderoga #2 pencil in hand. My request for college applications was proof of this. He had sent me applications for St. Joseph's University, Drexel University, Temple University, and Penn State. I had been away from home long enough that I cast aside the thought of Penn State and focused my attention on the other three universities in Philadelphia. An acceptance to any of these institutions meant that I could commute to school.

The question became, what did I want to study? Earlier in the previous year, I was awakened in the middle of the night and couldn't go back to sleep. Tossing and turning in my bunk for hours, I believed that God was calling me to be a pastor. Was this what I was supposed to do? I couldn't shake the thought that night and for several days afterward, but the idea gradually faded over the subsequent weeks.

Now, looking at the brochures spread out in front of me, the thought briefly returned. Should I be considering seminaries instead? As I leafed through the material, I found myself motivated by a strange and unrelated concept: a window sticker.

Driving around at home, it was not uncommon to see college students with stickers placed just above the trunk of their rear car windows, identifying where they were studying—Villanova, St. Joe's, Temple, Drexel, La Salle. While just three short years ago the thought of college terrified me, I now found myself wanting a sticker of my own. I was ready to be a college student. I had seen how the other half lived as an enlisted man in the United States Army. I was tired of being ordered around. I was tired of being cold, hot, and rained on. I was ready to exchange my rucksack for a book bag. The applications in front of me offered a world of opportunity. I enjoyed writing; maybe I should study journalism. As I pored over the available majors at Temple University, one struck me like a lightning bolt: Criminal Justice. I was intrigued by the classes offered in this major—Introduction to Criminal Justice, Criminal Law, Policing, Sex Crimes. All of it sounded exciting to me. No one in my family worked in the criminal justice system, so this was uncharted territory. I had a friend since elementary school whose father was a cop in Norristown. I had always thought he was so cool as he stood and watched our baseball games in his dark uniform and badge. I had joined the Army to serve our country, and my late-night calling to be a pastor suggested to me that my life of service was not yet complete. Perhaps my future was in law enforcement. This would allow me to serve others much closer to home while doing something meaningful and important. It seemed like a perfect fit. In that instant, I had found a major. The next phase of my life was shaping up, and I was heartened by the plan I was now putting into motion.

✳✳✳

The remaining eight weeks in Berlin were a blur of anticipation and preparation. We were subjected to a major inventory of all our gear during that time. This required us to lay out every piece of our equipment so that our Platoon Sergeant and Squad Leaders could visually verify that we still had possession of our gear and that it was in working order. This also included a walkthrough of our barracks room. Since only a select few of us had been chosen for deployment to Turkey, the majority of my platoon was unaware that I had snuck a cat home and was now hiding the fugitive in my barracks room. With help from my old infantry pal Ron, who was assigned to a different platoon and lived on the floor above me, we snuck Silopi out of the area until the inspections were completed. He brought down an empty box that his new television had come in, and we put Silopi inside. With no eyebrows raised, he took her to his room, where Uncle Ron got to kitty-sit until the coast was clear. It was another successful operation.

Time continued to tick by as I began the process of separating from the Army. I turned in my weapon and my equipment. I visited the personnel office to fill out volumes of paperwork. I arranged for the pickup and delivery of my household items, which consisted of little more than a stereo, a small TV, and a couple of duffle bags full of clothes. Additionally, I made flight arrangements for travel to Fort Dix, New Jersey, the primary out-processing facility for soldiers stationed overseas. Unlike my last flight, Silopi's travel to America would be legitimate and aboveboard. As with most of the federal government, the right hand has no idea what the left hand is doing. Thankfully, this meant that no one in the flight process asked why a single guy living in the barracks was traveling back to the United States with a cat. This time, she would be traveling in a plastic cat carrier kept in a special area for pets under the plane. My concerns about her being scared and alone during the flight were greatly alleviated by the peace of mind that came with knowing my arrest for secreting a cat across an international border was highly unlikely.

Days before my departure were spent saying goodbye to the guys I had spent so much time with over the months and years. One would think that this process would be similar to the final days of high school, when teenage girls ran to one another with giant hugs and even bigger tears, signing yearbooks and promising to stay in touch. But guys do not operate in quite the same way. Instead, there were handshakes and "Take cares." A quick change in global circumstances could have meant that, at any moment, you might be laying down your life for any of these men, or vice versa. Still, the constant turnover of personnel and duty stations tended to mute any real heartfelt emotions about leaving. They used to refer to American soldiers as G.I.s, an abbreviation for "Government Issue." As I prepared to depart, it really did feel as if that was what we were—government-issued troops. We were essentially living, breathing pieces of military equipment that Uncle Sam set around the world like pieces on a chessboard. Despite the time and experiences we all shared together, when it was your turn to leave, it simply meant that you would soon be replaced by another body wearing the same uniform and sporting the same haircut. It was not emotional; it was just the end of your time.

***

On my last day, Silopi and I were driven to the airport by my Lieutenant. This was a job he volunteered to do. In the military, there is an imaginary but distinct line between officers and enlisted men. This is emphasized by the requirement that officers be addressed as "Sir" and saluted whenever you pass them. Generally speaking, the only interaction between the two groups involved the officers passing down orders to enlisted men. In my experience, the two groups never hung out together, nor did they eat together. I suppose it is a separation that is necessary to maintain proper command and control. That is what made those several months living in a tent in Turkey with the Captain and the Lieutenant so unique, as well as my ability to tease them.

This mandated separation made the Lieutenant's offer to drive me to the airport all the more meaningful. I took his gesture of kindness to mean that he saw me as a man and not a subordinate. My suspicions were confirmed as we exited his vehicle at the airport and he extended his hand.

"Brad, it's been a pleasure," he said, shaking my hand. "You're a good man."

The use of my first name was a bit of a shock, especially coming from an officer. Over the last two years and 14 weeks, I had been known simply as "Beyer."

"Sir, I cannot thank you enough," I said.

"Chris," he replied, correcting me.

I was touched by his suggestion that I address him by his first name. More than 32 years later, I still remember this exchange; it marked a transition from boyhood to manhood, from soldier to human. In that moment, I was not a soldier, a grunt, or a Specialist E-4; I was just a man. I was being recognized as more than just a rank; I was being acknowledged as a person. He saw beyond my uniform and unexpectedly placed me on his level, and I appreciated it more than he could possibly know.

"Chris," I said, shaking his hand. "Thank you for everything."

"Keep in touch," he said with a clap on my back.

I picked up my duffel bag and Silopi's carrier and made my way into the airport terminal. I was heading home with a sense of confidence I did not think was possible three years earlier. I had made it through my time. I didn't quit. And now Silopi and I were heading home to the United States. Having been accepted to Temple University weeks earlier, it was time to face my old fear: college. My first semester was just a few weeks away.

13

BACK HOME (SORT OF)

The flight from Germany to the United States with Silopi was obviously much more relaxing than our last flight together. For starters, we were not violating any international laws or treaties. That fact certainly kept my pulse within the normal range. Luckily for Silopi, this trip did not involve being smooshed into an olive drab canvas hip purse for hours on end. This time, the airline was actually aware of her presence on the flight. Unfortunately, while my stress level was consistent with that of an ordinary air traveler, hers was probably off the charts, as she was placed in a holding area under the plane. For months, whenever she was subjected to an uncomfortable situation, she was with me—traveling from Turkey, trips to the vet and the shots that came with them, hiding her from prying eyes within the barracks; I was with her through all of it. As such, I was undeniably a source of comfort for her. Most children feel at ease in the presence of their parents, after all. But for now, the poor thing was stuck in a holding cell below a jet, certainly wondering where on God's green acre she was heading now.

As we flew, I could not help but reflect on all that had transpired in a little more than two years. I was returning home a different person. The Jersey Shore no longer seemed like a faraway destination. My first job at Kmart was no longer the epitome of breaking out on my own. Friendship no longer meant someone you went to elementary school with. Manhood no longer meant the ability to grow facial hair or hanging a high school diploma on your wall.

At the time, it was hard to say whether I loved or hated the Army. I just missed my home. I missed my family. Regardless of the exact nature of my feelings for the Army at that moment, I was most assuredly grateful to it. Like most of life's difficult undertakings, when you are in the midst of your misery and discomfort, it seems like your condition will never change. The pain will continue until you die. Then, with each passing day, you come to realize that you are stronger than you thought you were. You had to be, or you would not have made it through the previous day. Then somehow, the days clump together to form weeks and then months. You look up to see that the road behind you is much longer than the road you have yet to travel. Next thing you know, it's all over. Sitting in my seat, staring out at the fading European sky, I reached the realization that most of us come to experience as we reflect on our trials and tribulations: I guess it really wasn't that bad. Ingeniously, God grants us rose-colored glasses with which to view our pasts. This gift allows us to survive and move forward.

***

Landing in the United States felt like a blessing. It is easy to take for granted the comfort that comes with knowing that everyone around you speaks the same language, eats the same foods, and operates under the customs you are used to. The fact that it was only a couple of weeks before Christmas made the atmosphere of the airport that much more exciting. I had not been home for nearly a year, and to be only a state away from my family was a tremendous feeling. Thankfully, I would be seeing them in only a matter of hours.

As the other overseas soldiers and I collected our luggage, a Fort Dix representative was already hustling us along. We still had to be driven to the out-processing center to sign the last of our paperwork that would once again make us civilians, and apparently, the person tasked with getting us there was in a hurry. While my inflight ruminations about the Army seemed mixed, the rush we felt to get on the bus pushed my feelings firmly back into the "hate" camp. I was not going to miss the incessant barking and hurry that seemed to permeate this organization.

My urgency was intensified by the fact that I still had to collect my little girl. Luckily, when I arrived at the area where live animals could be retrieved, Silopi was already waiting for me. As I picked up her carrier, she began to chirp loudly. Most cats meow, but Silopi chirped instead. It was a string of staccato beeps like the Morse code messages you would hear in old movies: BEEP-BE-BEEP-BEEB-BE-BEEP. She was really giving it to me with both barrels. My mind instinctively translated her chirps: 'Do you know where I've been? They stuck me under the airplane. I had no idea where you were. I was scared. You weren't there. Now I'm hungry.'

"I know. I know," I said as I held up her carrier to meet her gaze.

Seeing my face seemed to calm her down for the time being. We were reunited, but in a hurry. As we made our way through the airport, following the group ahead of us, some people peeled off to quickly get some American fast food that beckoned them as they passed. As I write this now in my adulthood, I don't know what I was thinking at the time. I should have packed some food for her. Why didn't I bring a baggie with some dry cat food? In a world where people go for walks with a tumbler of coffee in their hand and their children can't make it through a 10-minute car ride, a church service, or even a line at Disney without a baggie of Pepperidge Farm Goldfish, Cheerios, or Cheez-Its being stuffed into their hands, it may seem hard to believe that I was not more prepared for the trip from Europe to the United States. However, being that I was twenty years old and relatively new to the feline father game, my foresight was obviously lacking.

With very few options, I found a sandwich shop and ordered Silopi a tuna hoagie. Desperate times call for desperate measures. Quickly, we joined the others heading for the exit as I opened her carrier and stuffed the tuna hoagie inside. The sandwich was as big as she was, but I could hear her gleefully chomping on the tuna as I sprinted to catch up. At least she was fed. Still, I could not stop grumbling about having just paid $7 for a sandwich. The things we do for our children.

***

Throughout my life, I have developed a means of dealing with the world known as 'defensive pessimism.' Having an eternal optimist as a father, I am not sure where I developed this unique worldview. Essentially, those who subscribe to the tenets of defensive pessimism assume that if two options are available, the worst will surely happen. Such a negative assumption helps inoculate the believer from potential disappointment. For example, if the Philadelphia Eagles had a fantastic first half against their division rivals, the Dallas Cowboys, an optimist would assume that the second half of the game will see the Eagles continue to increase their lead before going on to a triumphant victory. In contrast, the defensive pessimist approaches the second half with great trepidation, certain that the Birds will blow it in the fourth quarter. What is the benefit of such an approach, one might ask? Well, if the Eagles win, you'll be jubilant. If they lose... well, you knew it all along. In short, defensive pessimism helps protect the believer from the anguish and disappointment experienced by the cockeyed optimist. Some may call it being negative; I consider it preparing yourself for the worst.

Unfortunately, my defensive pessimism had not yet been perfected by the time I reached Fort Dix. Had it been, I would have been more prepared for what was heading my way. We were shown to a large barracks room with rows of bunk beds, not unlike my Basic Training barracks at Fort

Benning. It was interesting that we were going out the same way we came in—crammed into bunk beds with a bunch of people we didn't know. We were to spend the night and then be out-processed in the morning. I would then be heading home to my family in Norristown as a recovering infantryman.

No one had paid attention to the fact that I had Silopi in tow, and I was not about to single myself out when I was so close to being finished with the Army. You see, after two years and fourteen weeks of being constantly reminded that you were not special, I was not inclined to blurt out, "Hey, what should I do with my cat?" So, I found a bunk, stored my bags in the large wall locker at the head of the bed, and took Silopi in her carrier outside as I looked for a piece of ground where she could do her business. As I took her out of the carrier, she clung to me with wide eyes. It was clear that she had had enough.

"I know, baby. We're almost home," I said as I placed her on the ground.

I held onto her so that she did not try darting out into the dark and unfamiliar environment as she went to the bathroom in the grass. After putting her back in the carrier, we returned to the barracks room. I did not trust her to stay on my bunk with so many strange people surrounding us, so I decided to place her carrier in the wall locker, being sure to leave the door open for circulation. Not unlike the first night that I found her, the initial couple of hours were quiet and uneventful. But like that very same night when the Lieutenant had threatened to step on her head, Silopi came to life a few hours later. Her chirping grew louder and louder as I lay there in the darkness, praying that no one would hear her. My prayers went unanswered.

I could hear guys asking one another as they stirred, "What's that noise? Did you hear that?"

More and more people began to take notice, and I started to sweat. I was not in Turkey or Berlin anymore. There was no one to cover for me and my stowaway this time. Quietly, I got out of bed and removed her carrier from the wall locker. Crawling back into bed to avoid raising suspicion about my role in the nighttime interruption, I placed her carrier under my bunk. Lying on my stomach, I dangled my hand over the side of the bed and slipped several fingers through the hole of her carrier. Silopi's pink nose sniffed at my fingers, licked them, and then rubbed her nose against them.

"Oh, there you are," she seemed to say with these movements.

The slight reassurance my fingertips offered in this precarious situation seemed to be enough, and I could feel her settle down inside the carrier. She slept in blissful silence for the remainder of the evening as I lay there in the darkness, watching each hour tick away on the luminous dial of my watch. It felt like driving through the night in a truck loaded with nitroglycerin. You know there's a chance it could explode at any moment, but all you can do is pray that it doesn't.

✱✱✱

The blessed sunlight of the next day brought an end to my night watchman duties and the joy of impending discharge from the military. I watched as soldier after soldier was taken into various offices to sign paperwork before being transported to their waiting families at home. It was not unlike buying a car. You meet with the salesman to discuss price, and then you are escorted to the next office, where they try to upsell you on pinstriping and undercarriage protection. After that, you move to yet another office to sign additional paperwork. Finally, they drive your new car up to the door, and you depart, relishing that new-car smell while bemoaning the sixty months of payments that await you. However, unlike the car dealership experience, which brings a new sense of responsibility, the end of the Army out-processing experience brought with it a discharge of responsibility. Your time was up, and your tab was paid in full. You were no longer shackled to the U.S. military. I was mere minutes away from this feeling.

Finally, it was my time. Or so I thought. When I was called back into an office, I was informed that my paperwork had not been forwarded by the parties responsible at the Berlin Brigade. Since there was no internet, I would have to wait for this paperwork to arrive.

"How long will that take?" I asked.

"About a week," I was told before being booted from the office.

Had I been a full-fledged disciple of the defensive pessimism religion at the time, I would not have been surprised by this tersely delivered and utterly devastating news. Instead, I sat there and felt my internal organs erupt in a nuclear blast of disappointment. That was when I first became aware of a key reality in my life: if ten thousand people were given a brand-new Swiss wristwatch, mine would be the one with a broken minute hand. And thus, a defensive pessimist was born.

I was exhausted from being awake most of the night, worrying whether Silopi would break into another rousing midnight rendition of "I Am Woman, Hear Me Roar." As a result, the news that I was stuck for another week at Fort Dix was insufferable. I just wanted to go home. More importantly, I could not go on for another week trying to hide Silopi in a wall locker. There was only one person in my life I could call in a situation like this: I had to find a payphone.

***

"Good afternoon, Atlantic Concrete," the receptionist answered.

"Hi, can I speak to Bob Beyer, please?"

"Certainly," she said. "May I ask who's calling?"

"Yes, this is his son, Brad."

"Just a moment; let me see if he's in."

When the chips were down, my parents were always miracle workers. However, unlike my mother, my dad had a driver's license. This made his miracle-working abilities significantly more mobile.

"Hello, Brad James," my father belted out as he answered the phone.

"Hey, Pop. How are you?"

"Good, son. Are you on your way home?" The excitement in his voice was undeniable.

"Nope. I have a bit of a problem. The Army lost my paperwork. I have to stay here for at least another week until they get it. I can't keep the cat here. I hate to ask this, but is there any way you can come and pick her up and take her home with you?"

In typical fashion, my father responded to my request in four simple words: "I'll be right there."

Thankfully, his office was only about forty-five minutes from Fort Dix. I got him the information on where he needed to go, and before I knew it, I saw him walking toward the barracks in his clothes dressed, whistling. The number of times I've seen this tiny man walk in my direction in his shirt, tie, and sports coat cannot be counted. As children, when we played with the neighbor kids up the street, he would often be directed by my mother to walk up the block and retrieve us for dinner when he got home from work. As we played kickball in the side yards or rolled down the small hills in front of the houses, I could hear his distant whistling as he strolled up the sidewalk in his shirt and tie. When our eyes met, he'd make an exaggerated swing of his arm to let us know we should head home for supper. He would then stroll back home, whistling as he walked.

During baseball games, I would look over from shortstop to see him leaning against the third baseline fence in his shirt and tie. After football practices, as I walked from the field carrying my helmet, I would see him strolling in my direction, whistling. I never saw the man in jeans, and to be honest, I'm not sure how many times I've actually seen him in shorts. Perhaps it's a generational thing. For many, a good job today is considered one in which you don't have to wear a shirt and tie. Back then, it was the exact opposite. My dad had worked so many menial jobs for such low pay throughout his life that I think having a job in which he was expected to dress professionally was a source of pride for him. Now, as for his constant whistling—that's up for debate. One time, while walking through a store and whistling, my dad heard a little girl ask her mother, "Why is that man whistling, Mommy?" The woman replied, "I don't know, honey. Maybe he's nervous." This memory always made my dad chuckle. I can tell you, I've never seen him nervous. I think he was just a happy guy with a song forever in his heart.

And now, that same happy man was whistling and strolling in my direction. His presence was like a Coast Guard helicopter approaching a sinking fishing boat, and I was so thankful for his arrival.

As we met on the sidewalk, we shook hands. As I grew into a man, we rarely hugged. That was something he reserved for the women in his life and his grandchildren. For the men he loved, his handshakes came with a vigorous push-pull motion, as he attempted to knock you off balance. I received my push-pull right then and there. He never disappointed.

"Hiya, Brad James."

His greeting was routine and casual, as if he had just returned home from work, rather than greeting his son, whom he had not seen in nearly a year.

"Thank you so much, Pop. You're a lifesaver. She had me up all night." I then lifted the carrier so that he could see his new soon-to-be housemate.

"This is Silopi," I said, making the introduction.

"Hiya, Silopi," he said, looking into the carrier. "Your mother's already got some food and a litter box set up in the basement."

It seemed that my pet-loving mother had already made a compromise. Silopi could come home with me, but she would have to stay in the basement. This was going to be interesting. There were almost no finished basements in Norristown. Most of the homes were rowhouses and duplexes, so the basements were utilitarian. Ours had a concrete floor that my mother had painted so many times that we actually lost square footage. The walls were also concrete. The heater sat at one end of the narrow basement, while the other end had a small patch of indoor/outdoor carpeting, allowing us to play with our toys without freezing our lower extremities on the concrete floor.

The age of our home could be identified by two key features. The first was a large oil tank that held hundreds of gallons of home heating oil, re-filled periodically from the outside of the house by a long hose from an oil delivery truck. The second telltale sign of the home's age was hidden behind a door near the bottom of the steps. This rarely opened door led to a room strategically located closest to the alley and was referred to as the coal cellar. Before the installation of the oil tank, coal would be dumped through the outside hatch on the back patio, allowing the homeowner to heat the home in the early 1900s. For years, my younger brother and I had begged my mother to let us use this magical and rarely viewed part of the basement as a clubhouse. Unfortunately, the room was so damp and dank that it not only prevented any extended visits but also left you with the certainty that it was Edgar Allan Poe's motivation for writing "The Pit and the Pendulum."

In short, Silopi was not going to like her new home in our basement. But, as the old adage says, beggars can't be choosers. I got Silopi home to Norristown. It was up to her whether she would be able to charm her way onto the main floor.

After thanking my dad yet again for his mercy mission, I watched as he carried my feline companion off. He held the carrier up several times to peer inside at her as he walked. My dad was a lover of animals, but I could tell he was curious about the wild Turkish cat he now had in his possession. I was not worried about him; Silopi would win him over easily. It was my mother I was concerned about.

***

Later that night, I called home to thank my dad for being there for me once again and to see how the delivery had gone. My mom had me laughing out loud as she painted the scene for me.

My dad had made it home after Silopi had cried for over an hour and a half while sitting in the carrier on the back seat of his car. For any normal man, this would have been enough to toss the carrier onto the Pennsylvania Turnpike, but my dad was not a normal man. When he walked in the back door, my younger brother Eric took the carrier from him and, per my mother's instruction, carried it down to the basement. My mom and dad then took up protective positions sitting on the steps. This perch allowed them to peer through the railing to witness the unveiling of the potentially dangerous creature my father had just brought home. Eric, on the other hand, placed the carrier in the middle of the indoor/outdoor carpeting along the steps. Sensing that the mighty beast might need to use the restroom and unwilling to begin their relationship with an accident beyond her control, my mom had earlier placed a newly purchased litter box nearby.

As if lighting an industrial firework, Eric unlatched the top of the carrier, swung the lid open, and quickly joined my parents on the stairs. The three of them sat and watched, knowing that at any moment they might have to retreat up the stairs to safety if the wild creature decided to attack.

I laughed as I listened to her description of the evening's events. In response, my mom explained somewhat defensively, "Well, Brad, we don't know what a Turkish cat looks like."

The foolishness of their hesitation and clearly marked escape route became readily apparent when Silopi sat up on her haunches and calmly surveyed her new environment. There was no roar. There was no vicious swing of her mighty paw. Instead, she stretched her little body and made her way to the nearby litter box. Climbing into the dusty litter, she squatted and went to the bathroom for about five minutes. My parents and brother sat and watched with fascination. Silopi then moved to the food and water bowls and took a good helping of both. When she finished, she sat and looked at the three people who were staring intently back at her, both parties uncertain of what to do next.

When in doubt, my mom invariably turned to cleaning.

"Er, go get the carrier so I can wash it out," she said to my brother.

Eric cautiously made his way down the steps as he followed my mother's orders. Approaching the carrier like a firework that may or may not have gone off, he quickly retrieved the plastic container. You never know whether a Turkish cat is trying to lure you into a false sense of security before it attacks.

Taking hold of the carrier , my mother asked, "Why does this smell like tuna fish?"

I had not yet explained to her about my $7 airport tuna hoagie purchase. Walking up the steps to the kitchen, my mom closed the door to the basement so that the new arrival could not sneak upstairs and begin her path of destruction. Graciously, she left the lights on in the basement so that Silopi wouldn't be scared. Then, my mother engaged the security slide latch behind her, locking Silopi in. Though tiny and cute, my mom was not quite certain about the wild beast that had just been unleashed in her basement.

$$***$$

If I thought the reception station at Fort Benning was boring, I was woefully unprepared for my last week in the Army. With literally nothing to do but wait for paperwork that may or may never arrive, I tried to kill time by reading and playing an arcade game at a nearby convenience store. The days were excruciatingly long. It was like being a racehorse in the chute, waiting for the bell to ring and the gates to open. But the gates did not open for days. Was this the day? No. Maybe tomorrow. Nope. I then began to worry: what if my orders didn't come before Christmas? I felt pretty certain that I would be allowed to go home for the holiday, but with the way things were shaping up, who could be sure?

Then, seven days later, my paperwork finally arrived. I happily signed the documents that marked my release from the Army. I was not about to wait for their travel arrangements to be solidified, so, for the second time, I called my dad and asked him to travel from his office to Fort Dix, this time to bring me home. As anticipated, he was there in a flash, and we drove home together as two civilians.

14

HOME AGAIN (FOR NOW)

Walking in the back door, my house seemed extremely tiny. I'm not sure if it was an optical illusion or my brain's realization that I had tasted a world much larger than Norristown. As I entered the kitchen, the table that had always served as the center of the house seemed to have taken on the dimensions of the little white plastic stools they put in takeout pizza boxes to prevent the lid from smooshing the pizza. While I was incredibly grateful to be home, there was no mistaking the fact that I had grown during my time away. It was not a physical growth, but a growth born of experience and exposure. Though this was my home of record, in many ways it seemed like I no longer fit in it.

My mom hugged me in the kitchen. It seemed like just two weeks ago she had sat crying on my bed before I left. Curiously, it also felt like a decade earlier.

"Welcome home, Brad James," she said.

"It's good to be home," I smiled. Just then, my eternal hippie of a brother walked in and warmly greeted me in only the way he could: "Kill any babies today?"

Yep. It was good to be home.

Just then, a little black and white streak came zipping in from the living room as she heard my voice. It was

Silopi, and she began making figure eights around my feet in excitement. I scooped her up into my arms as she nuzzled into my neck. We were reunited once more, her body language seeming to scream out, "You're back. I missed you so much."

As I held her, I looked at my mom inquisitively. "What happened to keeping her in the basement?"

My mom gave a tiny shrug as she explained the reasoning behind her change of heart. "Well, it seemed so cold and lonely down there for her."

It appeared that in our week-long separation, Silopi had already won her over. That was impressive. The fact that she hadn't run away or been accidentally frozen to death by my mother in my absence was even more impressive. Christmas was truly a time of miracles.

***

As I entered the living room, the smell of pine enveloped me. We had always gotten a live tree, and this year was no different. My mother's ability to decorate was unmatched. While I had begged her over the years to have a "normal" tree with colored lights that twinkled and a mismatch of ornaments, there was no such luck. She was artistic and talented, and our Christmas trees always reflected her abilities. One year, the tree might be decorated with toile and baby's breath, while the following year she might decorate with a mother-of-pearl color palette. Keep in mind, these are all things that, as a man, I should have no idea what they mean. But this is what happens when you have a creative mother who works part-time at a craft store. For years, I had teased her that mauve is not a traditional Christmas color, but our input as the children of the house was neither requested nor necessarily appreciated. Still, I have to admit that her Christmas trees were always a work of art.

Now that Silopi was an official member of the family and her sweet temperament granted her access to the house above the basement level, two new Christmas traditions were born. The first involved the incessant, yet secretive, removal of the lowest Christmas ornament. Not surprisingly, once Silopi started living with us, we frequently returned home to find a single Christmas ornament lying alone in the middle of the living room floor. While it was distinctly possible that a good-natured poltergeist had accompanied Silopi from her humble beginnings in Turkey and had now taken up residence in our home, in reality, the explanation was much simpler and far less terrifying. It seemed that my feline daughter would wait until she was alone in the house before attacking the lowest ornament on the tree. She was smart enough to never let us see her do it, but I can imagine that she must have attacked that low-hanging ball like Rocky Balboa on the speed bag during a training montage. I've heard stories of cats climbing Christmas trees and toppling them over. Luckily for her sake, Silopi was not destructive. But I guess even she could not resist her inner feline urges. Strangely enough, my mom would continue to put the ornament in the exact same place each time. I took this to mean, "Well, there's no harm if she likes to play with it." It was a telltale sign that my mother was becoming a closet animal lover.

The second new Christmas tradition that accompanied Silopi's arrival into our family also involved the Christmas tree. Despite having a full water bowl at her disposal at any given moment, Silopi soon learned that the Christmas tree stand housed a little basin of water to keep the tree from drying out. Maybe it was the piney flavor of this water that drew her attention, but she developed a habit of drinking from the stand. For us, it meant having to repeatedly refill the water. For her, it meant that when she went number two in her litter box, little brown nuggets with pine needles sticking out in every direction were left behind. They looked like little spiky instruments of medieval torture. They could not have felt good coming out, but from that point forward, their presence meant that the Christmas season was in full bloom.

***

Many people tend to remember a specific Christmas by a particular gift they received. For the Christmas of 1991, my most memorable gift was a fuzzy maroon blanket emblazoned with a white "T." It was the logo for Temple University, the school I would be starting in a little more than a week. Despite surviving the Army, the gift still brought with it a sense of panic. I was going to college after the start of the new year. The thought and the gift made my stomach flutter. The reason why remains a strange mystery. The thought of leaving for Basic Training made me stop and think, but the thought of starting college made me panic. Luckily, the sight of Silopi batting around balls of discarded wrapping paper took my mind off the start of this new phase of my life. It seemed for many months now that she had a unique ability to provide a much-needed distraction when my mind needed it most.

The days moved faster as my start date approached. This caused the holiday season to fly by, and before I knew it, it was the night before my first day of college. Like every night since I returned home, Silopi followed behind me as I made my way upstairs to bed. Despite having three other people in the house, it was clear that Silopi belonged to me. As I crawled into bed, I felt her jump up after me. Lying there in the darkness and thinking about college, I had a realization. Having lifted weights and run so religiously before joining the Army, I was confident that my body would not let me down. I would be able to handle whatever the Drill Sergeants dished out. College, on the other hand, left me with many questions. Was I up to the challenge academically? Would I be smart enough? If college proved too difficult and I had to drop out, what would my next option be? I did not want to struggle like my parents did. I did not want money to be a constant worry in my life. As I saw it, a college education was the primary vehicle to ensure that would not happen. But was I truly up to the challenge?

Another concern was my current position in life. It felt so good to be home; that was certain. However, I felt different. My boyhood home—and, in fact, my boyhood bed—no longer felt like mine. I had experienced a world far larger than Norristown. I had lived an independent life. While I had been desperate to return home, it seemed impossible to put that toothpaste back in the tube. I was a little kid when I first lived in this home before the Army. Now, it felt artificial to be in the same environment as a man.

I have heard it said that you can't go home again. At that moment, I was certain of the truth behind this old adage. My life was different now. I was different now. The place was the same, but I wasn't. What should have felt like a return to normalcy felt more like a layover until the rest of my life began. But what would that final destination be? As all of this swirled around in my head, Silopi batted at the sheets and demanded entry. I lifted the covers, and she slid underneath, taking up her usual nighttime position. The stress did not seem to impact her in the least.

15
COLLEGE

Having had a half-day of orientation shortly before the start of classes, I was at least somewhat familiar with the campus of Temple University. It was certainly an urban campus. Temple is situated on 46 acres in North Philadelphia, intersected by Broad Street. Although it has various other campuses, approximately 10,000 students attend the main campus in Philly. The perimeter of the school's area is outlined by maroon flags bearing the Temple "T," which hang from buildings and light poles. As new students, we quickly learned that it was a far safer area within the confines of the flags than it was outside of them. In light of the crime that exists largely beyond Temple's boundaries and too frequently seems to seep in, Temple University has the largest university police force in the United States. Despite the efforts of the department's 130 officers, crime has always managed to make its way inside the imaginary perimeter. This became apparent to me when I returned to my car after the first day of class to find the antenna ripped off my vehicle. It seemed that parking along the street on campus, instead of in the paid student parking lots, was not advisable. I made this same mistake many months later.

Because I had not obtained the requisite parking tokens to access one of the sanctioned parking lots that day, I parked immediately outside a student lot safely tucked behind a barrier of chain-link fencing. I rolled the dice, believing I would only be in class for a few hours. My gamble failed miserably; when I returned to my vehicle, I found my driver's side window smashed and the interior ransacked. As I surveyed the damage, the guard in a small booth inside the student lot, approximately thirty yards away, yelled out to me, "They also took your golf clubs out of your trunk."

I walked to the trunk and lifted it; it had already been unlatched by the long-gone culprits. Sure enough, my golf clubs had also been stolen. "Thanks a lot," I yelled back, giving the useless guard a wave. "Did you help them load my clubs into their car?" I asked.

Mr. Useless just shrugged and went about his day as I drove home with the wind screaming in through my broken side window.

I soon learned that it was much easier and far more convenient to take the train from Norristown to Temple each day. This not only removed the stress of traversing the Schuylkill Expressway but also afforded me time to get a jump on reading class materials as I headed to and from school. Since the Elm Street Station was the last stop on the Manayunk/Norristown Line, it was also possible to catch a nap on the way home each afternoon without the fear of missing my stop.

***

Right from the outset, I enjoyed Temple as much as a college student can. Commuting each day made it feel like a job rather than being stuck on campus. Unfortunately, the first day of classes each semester always seemed to bring a certain sense of anxiety. As the professors explained the expectations for the course and the work required, I would listen and think, "There's no way I'm ever going to be able to do this."

Quizzes, midterms, finals, papers, projects, attendance... hearing everything in one giant chunk felt overwhelming. Still, there was a certain sense of excitement to it as well. I was doing something none of my siblings had ever done. I was forking out the down payment for the rest of my life.

Buying my required texts at the bookstore on the first day of classes was also a source of excitement. As I searched through the stacks for my textbooks, it felt real. I was facing my fear. On that very first day, as I placed my hand on my first college book, I saw it: hanging in a display was a row of window stickers. I picked one that read "Temple University" alongside the school's academic logo. I added it to my purchase and later affixed it to the rear window of my car. I was not only proud; it was now official. I was a college student.

Luckily for me, paying for school was not an impediment. The G.I. Bill ensured that. When I first enlisted in the Army, I did not sign up for the G.I. Bill. There was no point; I had enlisted to avoid college. However, after a couple of weeks of Basic Training, our drill sergeant gathered us in front of the barracks and touted the benefits of the G.I. Bill. He advised that if we wished to start the paperwork to enroll in this important program, now would be the time. At that point, I had already observed enough of Army life to keep my options open, so I decided to fill out the requisite paperwork to enroll in the G.I. Bill. It would prove to be one of the best decisions I ever made. Now, attending Temple University, I was able to pay my tuition and books and still had about a thousand dollars left over each semester. I was proud that my parents didn't have to pay for me, not that they could have even if they wanted to. Even more importantly, college meant much more to me since my prior military service was footing the bill for my current education.

***

As I returned home from college each afternoon, Silopi was there to meet me at the door. Throughout the day, she would find various spots around the house to take her numerous naps. One of her prime locations was on the third floor of our home. My mom said she could always tell when my car pulled into the alley because she would hear Silopi's frantic footfalls reverberating like a bass drum as she dashed from the third floor to the second floor and down the front steps in a mad clamor to greet me at the back door. We never knew how she could tell that my car was approaching from such a significant distance, but she always seemed to do so.

Having a tendency to do my reading and homework while lying face down on the floor, I found that Silopi would immediately take up a position sitting on my backside. There, she would curl up in a ball and nap as I studied. As in the Army, we were always together, and she always kept a close eye on me.

Despite having my schooling paid for, I still felt the need to work. My first job as a teenager had been at our local Kmart. On the day I received my driver's license, I put on a shirt and tie and drove to the store to meet with a woman in human resources. After a brief discussion, I was hired as a stock boy and occasional cashier. I loved the stocking aspect of the job: setting up and tearing down displays, moving merchandise, carrying heavy items to customers' cars, and throwing out the putrid trash from the cafeteria. I loved being able to move about the store unfettered. Unfortunately, when the store got busy, I would too frequently hear a dreaded call over the loudspeaker:

"Clock 97 to checkouts please. Clock 97 to checkouts."

This call was like a sad and disappointing bat signal. It meant that I was needed to cover a register due to an influx of customers. This was the part of the job I detested—standing in one spot as a long line of customers spread out from my conveyor belt, each one needing to be rung up. It made me feel like a neglected dog chained to a decrepit front stoop. Being that it was 1987, most people used cash, which meant making correct change. Some people wrote checks, which meant waiting as they crossed their I's and dotted their T's. This also required me to check their driver's license against their freshly written check. When a customer occasionally whipped out a credit card,

I had to retrieve the old clunky contraption in which you placed a carbon copy slip over their credit card and slid the handle to make an imprint. Then, as was known to happen at Kmart, customers often arrived at the checkout with an item missing a price tag. This meant I had to sit and stare at the angry faces of customers as one of my fellow stock boys frantically searched the store for a matching product with an intact price tag. This undertaking was known by shoppers far and wide as the dreaded "price check." Not only could it be an excruciatingly long process, but it also meant the lines grew longer as the faces became more and more sour.

I knew that I hated working the register, but I didn't quite realize how much anxiety it had caused me beneath the surface. The depths of my misery became clearer after a dream I had one night. In my dream, I was working at the checkout in the exact same situation. As I sat and waited for what seemed like an hour for the price check, I began to apologize to the customers for the delay. As I waited and waited for the unspecified stock boy to return with a price, I started to grow tired. My fatigue became so overwhelming that I decided to lie down in the checkout lane. I apologized to the customers for my overwhelming need for rest and asked them to kindly wake me when my coworker returned with the correct price for the item. My level of guilt for taking a nap at my register was outweighed only by my uncompromising fatigue.

When my dad woke me up for school the next morning, he was shocked by the condition of my bed. "What happened?" he asked in disbelief. He walked into my room to find me lying on a bed completely devoid of any bedclothes. Instead, my flat sheet and fitted sheet had been folded neatly and placed in my pillowcase. I woke up freezing and immediately remembered my dream. Apparently, I had engaged in an act of sleep cashiering. I must have scanned my own sheets, folded them, placed them into what I thought was a shopping bag, and then sat on the end of my bed waiting for a price check on my own sheets until I could no longer resist the sweet temptation of sleep. I think it is safe to say that I really did not like working the register.

*****

Despite the hell of working the register, I loved the two years I spent working at Kmart as a teenager. It was not only a job but also a form of socialization. I became close friends with some of the employees there, and my first girlfriend worked there. Every shift led to a funny story or an interesting happening. Many of us ate meals together and teased one another. There were breakups and hookups, infighting and power struggles. It was a cut-rate Melrose Place before Melrose Place ever hit the airwaves. It therefore made sense that since I was back home again and in need of a part-time job, I should return to my previous occupational life. But just like you can't go home again, you also can't go back to Kmart again. When I returned, many of the faces I once knew and liked were gone. Even more disappointing was the fact that my new assignment did not involve stocking shelves. In fact, it didn't even involve me working a register. Instead, I was assigned to work in women's apparel. If I was disheartened in the Army to be moved from my infantry position to an ammunition specialist position, there are no words to define the dismay and humiliation of being assigned to stock women's dresses at Kmart. I still consider it a tremendous accomplishment that I lasted a month in this prison of cheap fabric before finding more meaningful employment.

Since one of my dad's part-time jobs was working as a bookkeeper for a local realtor and landlord, I found part-time work cleaning the office and the common areas of various apartment houses in downtown Norristown. I also got connected with a friend of my older brother who owned his own landscaping company. This led to recurring seasonal work that lasted throughout my college years: cutting lawns in the summer, splitting wood in the fall, and shoveling sidewalks in the winter. It was another job where co-workers became family and funny stories abounded. Above all, Silopi loved this job the most. The reason was quite simple. Every time I came home from work and threw my sweaty and dirty clothes in front of the washer, per my mother's instructions, Silopi would immediately find the stinky armpits of my shirts and roll around in them. I don't know if the smell reminded her of our time together in the Army, but she obviously loved the fragrance that followed me home after a long day of landscaping. She was cute; that part was undeniable. Her intelligence level, on the other hand... who can say?

***

As my first semester at Temple continued, I began to notice that my hard work and studying were beginning to pay off. My quizzes, tests, and assignments continued to result in A's. I showed up for classes, did the assigned readings, and studied. My default study method was notecards. Whenever I asked, my dad and I would lay on his bed, and he would quiz me on the notecards I made. Silopi would always join us for these study sessions, looking back and forth like a tennis match spectator as my dad asked the questions and I provided the answers. I would frequently set my alarm for two or three in the morning and take up residence at our kitchen table for one last round of notecards. I would then return to bed for a couple of hours before catching the train into the city. On these early morning wakeups, Silopi would dutifully follow me down the stairs to supervise my study habits. She was not pleased with the regimen, but she tagged along nonetheless. The hard work paid off. By the end of my first semester, my report card reflected all A's. I was thrilled. My father was even more so.

And so it went: semester after semester, A after A. I could not have been more pleased that my diligence was bearing great fruit. In fact, this was my prayer for much of my life: 'God, I promise to put in the hard work. I just pray that you let the hard work pay off.'

And He did, over and over again. My choice of a Criminal Justice major proved to be a perfect fit. I loved the material and enjoyed learning about the various aspects of the U.S. legal system. After taking and enjoying several psychology classes, I also decided to add Psychology as a minor. It only made sense.

From an academic standpoint, I was on cruise control. The weeks were passing by, and so were the semesters. I thought my future was set, but I failed to realize that there was a piece of the academic puzzle missing.

***

During the fall semester of my junior year, I was sitting in the classroom waiting for class to begin. Listening to some of my fellow Criminal Justice majors chat, I heard a word that I had not yet considered: "internship." I heard them talking about internship opportunities they were seeking at local law enforcement and probation agencies. I immediately felt behind the eight ball, and this panicked me. Growing up with my father and older brother, I was raised on competition. Whether it was ping pong, basketball, or even pitching pennies in the kitchen while my mom was at work, everything was a competition. As a result, I could not stand the thought that some of my classmates were ahead of me in the internship hunt, even though I hadn't realized that such a hunt was underway just minutes earlier. I had to get going. I could hardly wait to get home.

I rushed in the door but cut my daily reuniting with Silopi short. I needed to start my internship research as soon as possible. Since it was 1994, the internet had not yet been created to aid my research efforts. As such, I grabbed the greatest repository of information available to me at the time: the phone book.

Flipping to the blue pages in the middle of the phone book, I looked for a telephone number for the Federal Bureau of Investigation in Philadelphia. If I was going to seek out internship opportunities, it only made sense to start at the top and work my way down. Finding what I was looking for, I grabbed our house phone and dialed the number.

"Thank you for calling the Philadelphia Field Office of the Federal Bureau of Investigation..."

After listening to a series of prompts, I eventually reached an operator. I explained my inquiry, and she put me in touch with what they referred to as the Applicant Coordinator.

I informed the Applicant Coordinator that I was a Criminal Justice major at Temple University and was curious whether the FBI had an internship program. As most of us can attest, timing is everything. I was informed that not only did the FBI have an internship program, but they were currently accepting applications. This was great news that immediately set my juices flowing. They collected my information and agreed to mail me a packet with the application and requirements.

A few days later, I received a packet that outlined the FBI's Honors Internship Program and the application process. Included in the packet was an SF-86, Questionnaire for National Security Positions. I immediately placed the document into my Brother word processor, which had carried me thus far through my college career. Typing in my information, careful keystroke after careful keystroke, I began the laborious process of completing the all-encompassing background application. This required in-depth information about my parents, my siblings, my references, my places of employment, and so on. I had to start ordering transcripts, getting headshots, and writing an essay explaining my interest in the program. It was a lot of work, but the thought of once again working for the federal government, this time in a civilian capacity, was an exciting proposition. I was energized and motivated, and I sent my application packet in well before the deadline. Having dealt with the federal government as a much younger man, I now knew that all I could do was sit back, try to relax, and play the waiting game.

16

THE BUREAU

I finished the fall semester of 1994 with another perfect report card, and the spring semester of 1995 was similarly off to a strong start. Because the wheels of the federal government turn so incredibly slowly, there had been no word from the FBI in months. Then, as winter began to yield to spring, I received perhaps the most exciting piece of mail in my 23 years on the planet. The return address identified the letter as originating from the FBI in Washington, DC. As I tore into the envelope, I quickly learned that I had been selected for the FBI Honors Internship Program in Washington, DC, for the summer of 1995. It was a paid position lasting from June to August. The letter was quickly followed by telephone calls from the Philadelphia Field Office. I was directed to report to the FBI office in the federal building in Philadelphia to undergo drug testing, fingerprinting, and a polygraph examination. The wheels were turning rapidly, and my head was spinning just as fast.

Donning a suit and catching the train to Philadelphia, I made my way to the federal building. As I sat in the lobby waiting for my pre-employment polygraph, I observed Special Agents coming in and out of the office. I couldn't help but wonder what it would be like to have such an important job. This thought transported me to a distant place filled with wonderful musings. For now, however, I was more than happy just to be considered for the intern position.

My day at the FBI office proved to be a whirlwind. The fingerprinting was interesting, the polygraph was terrifying, and the opportunity to chat with the Special Agent in Charge of the Philadelphia office was an honor. On the walk back to the train, my feet barely touched the ground as I marveled not only at what I had just experienced but also at what it could potentially mean for my future. It reminded me of my swearing-in at the Military Entrance Processing Station (MEPS) office in Philadelphia a short seven years earlier. Just like that experience, this day carried a similar weight of importance and the undeniable feeling that my life was about to change. I had no idea just how monumental that change would be.

✳✳✳

By that point in my college career, I had met a fellow Criminal Justice major who worked for a private investigator with an office in nearby Conshohocken. He pulled me aside and asked if I would like to participate in an operation his company was organizing. He explained that his boss had contracts with major companies like Nike, Coach, Disney, and Ray-Ban. Because these products were so heavily counterfeited, the private investigation company targeted local flea markets where knock-offs were often sold. Occasionally, these flea markets were so filled with counterfeits that the company would coordinate with federal, state, and local law enforcement to descend on the unsuspecting counterfeit peddlers, confiscating numerous trash bags full of their phony merchandise. At times, these counterfeit peddlers were also arrested, but more frequently, they were left holding a cease-and-desist letter in the middle of a now-empty sales booth. Since my fellow student was in search of extra manpower, I was asked to assist in an upcoming operation.

For a college student, this was an exciting proposition, and I readily accepted. I must have met the company's expectations because I was soon offered a position with them. This meant weekend trips to flea markets to scout for counterfeits. Even more thrilling was the opportunity to participate in surveillance operations. In addition to counterfeiting investigations, the private investigation company also conducted surveillance on behalf of insurance companies that suspected claimants of feigning injuries or filing false workers' compensation claims. Our goal was to try to catch these potential scam artists on video, limping and hobbling from their doctor's appointments in the morning, then golfing, playing tennis, or shooting hoops in the afternoon. It was a fun job that introduced me to the concept of covert surveillance and the indescribable joy of having a position that didn't confine me to an office throughout the workday.

My boss at the private investigation company was the first to inform me that a nice man from the FBI had stopped by the office to ask questions about me. Similar news soon followed from my boss at the landscaping company, a friend from Kmart, a neighbor, and my pastor. It appeared that the background check was in full swing. It was a bit unnerving to know that the FBI was digging into my background. Many of us have likely worried at some point in our lives about what others might be saying about us behind our backs. Knowing that the FBI was directly confronting people in my life with such questions turned this subconscious concern into outright fear. Still, as word trickled back to me after these interviews, it was clear that tremendous progress was being made in my background investigation.

***

Weeks later, I received a phone call that far surpassed the previous letter I had received from the Bureau. While doing homework on the floor of my bedroom with Silopi sitting in her usual position on my lower back, my mom entered the room to inform me that a woman from the FBI in Quantico was on the phone. Silopi jumped from my back as I raced to the phone. The incredibly friendly woman on the other end informed me that not only had my background check been completed, but I had been assigned to the Investigative Support Unit at the FBI Academy in Quantico, Virginia.

I soon learned that the Investigative Support Unit, or ISU, was the operational side of the Behavioral Sciences Unit. Essentially, I would be an intern working with behavioral profilers. Keep in mind, just four years earlier, the movie 'Silence of the Lambs' had been released, winning a slew of Academy Awards, including Best Actor, Best Actress, and Best Picture. This was the movie that put profiling on the map, and I had just been told that this would be my assignment for the summer of 1995. For a college student majoring in Criminal Justice and minoring in Psychology, this was the equivalent of being told that I had been selected to serve as the batboy during the World Series. I was thrilled beyond words. Silopi had taken up residence on my bed during the phone call and stared at me as if trying to piece together the news I was receiving. Thanking the woman for the call, I hung up the phone. Silopi then chased after me as I sprinted downstairs to share the amazing information I had just received.

***

A couple of months later, I packed up my Jeep Wrangler for the drive to Alexandria, Virginia, where the FBI had arranged housing for the 102 Honors Interns selected from across the country. I did not realize just how competitive the program was until I learned that so few of us had been chosen to participate.

My walks to and from the house to pack my car meant that I had to keep Silopi from dashing outside. She had developed the nasty habit of trying to escape as we entered and exited the back door. I don't think she actually wanted to escape; I think her curiosity about the magical outside world that everyone in the house kept going to each day was too overwhelming for her. If we sat outside on the back patio to enjoy the warm weather, we would occasionally take her with us on a tiny harness that we would stake into the ground. None of us were anxious to repeat the great turtle escape of 1981. Fortunately, she enjoyed lying on our small tuft of lawn, munching on the grass that poked up all around her.

Her black-and-white body, surrounded by the green grass of summer, made for a picture of contentment.

When it came time to bring her back in, she would chirp at us in her feline morse code, her way of voicing her displeasure. It was the same chirping we all received on those occasions when she had been accidentally locked in the basement.

"Where's Silopi?" somebody would ask when she hadn't been seen in a while.

The answer was usually the same: she must have snuck down to the basement when the door was accidentally left open. My mother had originally earmarked our cold and uninviting basement as Silopi's home upon her arrival from Germany; luckily for Silopi, this idea did not last long. However, our basement always seemed to beckon to her like a siren's song. Whenever the door was left open, her inner explorer drove her to investigate, leading to her being inadvertently locked in the basement. When someone unlocked the door to find her sitting at the top of the basement steps, they would be barraged with an earful of unhappy chirps.

The message was always the same: "Why did you lock me down there? I only went down for a minute, then someone locked me in. I sat at the top of the steps and waited and waited, but nobody came for me." Beep... B-Beep... B-Beep... Beep.

Having packed my suits and necessities in my Jeep, I held Silopi and said goodbye to my parents. Since the internship program was about ten weeks long, I realized at that moment that this would be the longest I had been away from Silopi since I found her nearly four years earlier. When she sat in my hat in the chow hall in Turkey, I was just a few months away from making the drastic transition from military life to civilian life. Setting her down and walking out of the house brought a very similar feeling. Granted, this was just a summer internship, but I felt like I was standing at the end of the diving board, staring down at the cool, clear water of the pool beneath me. I could sense that this next step was going to be significant. However, unlike my trip to Basic Training or my first day of college, this next step brought no fear. I felt no anxiety. As I sped down I-95 from Philadelphia to Washington, DC, with the roof off my Jeep, I felt nothing but the sun, the wind, and a beckoning sense of anticipation.

***

The internship was everything I had hoped for. Similar to my time in the Army, I met people from all over the United States. Both of my summer roommates were from the West Coast, and like me, they seemed driven. In fact, every intern I met that summer had not only a story of their past but also a plan for their future. It was motivating to be around people who were so motivated; the desire to succeed was contagious.

While the majority of the interns were assigned to units at the monstrous FBI Headquarters building in DC, a couple dozen of us were fortunate enough to be assigned to the FBI Academy located within the confines of the Marine Corps base in Quantico, Virginia. I immediately recognized the building from "Silence of the Lambs," and I would be lying if I said I was not starstruck by that fact. As I traversed the hallways each morning, I saw the new agents in training hustling past me in tan cargo pants and blue polo shirts. It took about thirty-five seconds of this experience to realize that I wanted to be one of them. For a place I had never visited, there was something about the FBI Academy that felt like home.

The Behavioral Sciences Unit was located a short elevator ride down to the basement. Again, the surroundings were exactly like those in the movie. The profilers we met and offered our services to could not have been kinder or more helpful. We were exposed to fascinating subjects that most people would run from. Topics like murder, sexual assault, blood spatter, threat assessments, and body disposal sites were daily fare in the unit, and I was captivated by all of it. I was personally tasked with identifying cases of mass homicide and then calling the investigating agencies to request copies of their case files. I reviewed and statistically analyzed their files and documented my results in a rather lengthy report. Perhaps it is sad and a little morose to say, but I found the entire process to be a little slice of heaven.

The work was incredibly interesting, and it was impossible not to feel blessed by the opportunity I had been given through both the internship and the unit I was fortunate enough to be assigned to. My brief tenure left me with a new goal in life: I needed to become a part of this organization. My sights were now set on one uncompromising destination: I wanted to be an FBI agent.

***

As wonderful as the internship was and the newfound motivation it brought, there was an even greater takeaway for me. Though unexpected, it ended up changing my life in ways I never thought possible. For the handful of us assigned to the Behavioral Sciences Unit and the Investigative Support Unit, we received an initial orientation during our first week. We sat and listened as various members of these units introduced themselves, explained their roles within the organization, and outlined our responsibilities for the summer. When one particular Unit Chief was introduced, I turned to the intern on my right and made a wisecrack about the man's last name. Sadly, as an incorrigible smart aleck, the pun was a simple reflex for me. It wasn't until I turned to share my comment with the neighboring intern that I realized who I was sitting next to. Seated to my right was a beautiful blonde in a brown business suit with white trim along the lapels. She had stunning green eyes complemented by a flawless smile. Had I been a decade older with children, my quip would have easily been identified as a "dad joke." Nonetheless, this gorgeous colleague laughed at my childish pun. As classy as she appeared in that room at the FBI Academy, she also seemed to have a sense of humor—or lack thereof—that could appreciate my lowbrow and uninspired wit.

Her name was Kristen, and she came from a faraway and magical-sounding land called Michigan. Having graduated from the University of Michigan, her Ford Explorer had a front license plate with a big yellow block letter "M" against a blue background. I was now able to identify this as the logo for the University of Michigan. Seeing the logo immediately took me back to the giant University of Michigan flag hanging in the soldier's room in Berlin when I first arrived at my new duty station. Back then, when I first saw this flag, I was about to embark on a new journey in Europe. Looking at Kristen's license plate now at the FBI Academy, I felt once again that I was on the verge of a new voyage in my life. In today's popular culture, the term "easter egg" refers to items hidden in a movie or video game for the enjoyment of those who hide them and those who discover them. As I write this story now, the presence of the University of Michigan flag at a time when my life was about to change drastically feels like God had secretly slipped His own little easter egg into my life.

***

While my first interaction with Kristen was unintentional, the following days brought about a slew of more deliberate meetings. I was fortunate to have been granted an office during the internship, while Kristen was assigned to a cubicle just down the hallway. Although I had excelled in college up to that point, it was surprising how many questions I had that only she seemed capable of answering. At the time, Kristen was a graduate student working on her Ph.D. in Clinical Psychology. With such an advanced level of education, I found myself heading to her desk throughout the day with a variety of psychological, statistical, and computer-related questions. Much to my pleasure, she was willing to answer my questions, no matter how ridiculous or deliberate they may have sounded. To my even greater delight, she routinely made her way to my office for quick chats that often ended with both of us laughing. Regardless of where our conversations took place, I could not get enough of them.

These meetings at work soon led to meetings at our apartment complex. We would sit by the pool and discuss our lives, our families, and our love of movies and classic television. We bonded over an incessant volley of movie quotes and Brady Bunch trivia. I shared with her my toddler stage when I referred to my family only by Brady Bunch names, and she laughed. I imitated the cast of the classic "Rudolph the Red-Nosed Reindeer" Christmas special we both watched as children, and she laughed. Given where we were working that summer, she would imitate Clarice Starling while I would imitate Hannibal Lecter, and we both laughed.

She seemed particularly moved by my having served in the Army. Apparently, she had not known anyone who had served their country in such a manner. This topic led me to recount my experience of finding Silopi, sneaking her back to my barracks in Berlin, and eventually moving her to my home in Norristown. This story seemed to resonate with her even more.

For many guys, talking to a girl as beautiful as Kristen would bring a sense of worry over saying the wrong thing or sounding foolish. However, she was so sweet, kind, and down-to-earth that it felt like I was talking to a girl I had been friends with for years, rather than someone I had met only a week earlier. She exhibited a rarely seen combination of being both interesting and genuinely interested. Perhaps best of all, when she was not in business attire for work, she wore a baseball hat. While I had dated girls in the past, none of them wore baseball hats. For many guys, this last point is significant. There is nothing more attractive than a woman in a baseball hat. In fact, I had joked over the years that if given the choice, I would have my bride in a baseball hat with a veil that ran along the brim.

Our talks eventually led to a first date, and then another, and then another after that. Throughout the summer, we became inseparable. We traveled to places like Baltimore's Inner Harbor, the Naval Academy, Virginia Beach, and Ocean City, New Jersey. The trip to Ocean City was particularly significant, as I introduced Kristen to my love of the Jersey shore and to some of my family, who just happened to be vacationing there at the time. The more we talked and the more time we spent together, the more we realized how much we had in common. In countless ways, she was just like me.

Fans of the television show "Seinfeld" may recall the episode in which Jerry finds a woman who shares all of his same traits. He then explains to his neighbor Kramer, "Now I know what I've been looking for all these years. Myself. I've been waiting for myself to come along. And now I've swept myself off my feet!" Though a funny scene, in our case, Jerry Seinfeld's words rang completely true. We were a perfect match, and this realization made our relationship different from any other. We joked that the FBI's Honors Internship Program had turned out to be the world's greatest dating service. Not only did we share the same values, but we had each gone through a lengthy background check, a drug test, fingerprinting, and a polygraph examination just to get there. I can assure you, FarmersOnly.com does not offer that level of service to its customers.

As in the rest of my life, it appears that God had a role in all of this as well. While I had applied for the internship in the fall of 1994, Kristen had actually tried to apply in the fall of 1993. Fortunately for both of us, she learned about the internship three days after the closing date, meaning she would have to wait until the following year to apply. I took this as more than mere luck. But the signals of divine intervention did not stop there. On one of our first dates, we went to a funky little pizza place for dinner. After ordering our meals, Kristen excused herself to go to the ladies' room. As I saw her walking back to the table, I was surprised to see her wearing a wedding dress. The vision lasted only a brief moment before she returned to the clothes she had been wearing when she left the table. Now, I have never hallucinated in my life, either up to this point or at any point since. However, people often say, "You just know when you know." If there is any truth to this claim, then I had just been educated with a sledgehammer.

✳✳✳

As the internship began winding down, our relationship became an understandably routine topic of conversation. We were both operating under the deeply held belief that our time together had been more than a summer fling. Still, the logistical reality that our homes were six hundred miles apart was an obvious stumbling block. To expand our time together a little longer, Kristen asked me to return with her to Michigan to attend her brother's upcoming wedding in August. The idea was brilliant, and I readily agreed. It would give us another week together before we both returned to college in the fall.

At the end of the internship program, we had a banquet as a final send-off. This event afforded us the opportunity to meet and take pictures with the FBI Director, Louis Freeh, a tremendous honor for a group of interns. I was selected by the other interns to speak on behalf of our group during the banquet, and I thanked everyone at the FBI for giving us all an experience of a lifetime. I ended the speech by addressing the FBI Director, stating that hopefully the next time we all got a chance to see him, he would be handing us our credentials at a New Agents graduation ceremony. I walked away from the internship program that day with a new direction, a new goal, and a new girlfriend whom I was absolutely crazy about.

Kristen followed me as we drove to Norristown to drop off my car before heading to Michigan. While she had already met my parents at the Jersey Shore earlier that summer, this was her first time meeting Silopi. Entering the house, Silopi bolted for me as usual. Holding her in my arms, Silopi made Kristen's acquaintance. Kristen told me that my story of rescuing Silopi was one of the things that made her fall in love with me. As such, having the two of them meet proved to be a surprisingly meaningful moment.

Driving to Kristen's home in Michigan the following day was equally meaningful. On our nine-hour drive together, we listened repeatedly to what became the soundtrack of our summer: the "Cracked Rear View" album by Hootie and the

Blowfish, the "Jagged Little Pill" album by Alanis Morissette, and my East Coast contribution, "Billy Joel's Greatest Hits." These were the songs we had fallen in love to, and our westward drive brought the joy of having successfully eked out another week together. Sadly, underlying this adventure was the sobering realization that our time together would soon be coming to a close. Like a vacation, you knew that despite your best efforts, the days would tick by faster than you wanted them to, and unfortunately for us, our future together was more than uncertain.

***

As we exchanged the rocky, narrow passes of the Pennsylvania Turnpike for the flat expanses of the Ohio Turnpike, I was amazed by the wide-open feel that the Midwest offered. The Pennsylvania Turnpike transitioned from the congestion of the tightly packed and industrial Philadelphia area to the congestion of the mountainous and industrial Pittsburgh area. Yet, Ohio seemed wide and flat as far as the eye could see. The difference between the two states felt like an asthmatic taking a panicked hit of their inhaler. Driving through the Midwest, I felt like I could breathe again.

Turning north into Michigan continued this sense of openness. I was amazed to find that the surface streets around Kristen's home were wider than most of our expressways in the Philadelphia area. As we neared her home, every turn revealed inland lakes of various sizes. People were waterskiing, tubing, and puttering around in something I had never seen before—pontoon boats. Despite being a northwestern suburb of Detroit, the constant view of lakes gave the area a laid-back vacation feel. It reminded me of crossing over the bridge into Ocean City, New Jersey, knowing that the fun of swimming and fishing awaited on the other side.

Kristen's childhood home, though only slightly more than 2,100 square feet and set on just shy of a half-acre of immaculately manicured lawn, felt like a mansion to me. Her best friend growing up lived on a lake just down the road, and Kristen had spent her summers there swimming, sunbathing, and boating. It could not have been more different than Norristown.The houses were predominantly positioned in something called subdivisions rather than blocks. There were no sidewalks in front of their homes, and streetlights were few and far between. Even the addresses sounded different. In Norristown, you lived on a "street" that formed a block with other streets running perpendicularly at right angles, such as Marshall Street, Stanbridge Street, Oak Street, and Elm Street. If you didn't know the exact address of a person, you at least knew what "hundred block" they lived on. In contrast, the roads around Kristen's neighborhood ended with words like "Lane," "Court," "Trail," or "Drive." There were no blocks or right angles; instead, the roads gently snaked around the various lakes that dotted the landscape. It was safe to say that I fell in love with Michigan instantly.

As I pulled Kristen's Explorer into her driveway, she leapt from the vehicle and made a mad dash for the door connecting her garage to the house, yet another difference between the houses in Michigan and Norristown. She was met at the door by her mother, who seemed to have bolted toward the same door at the same speed once she saw Kristen's vehicle pull up. She had not seen her little girl in months, and her excitement at the reunion was palpable.

When Kristen's mom ripped the door open, her appearance took my breath away for just a moment. Like her daughter, she was also a beautiful blonde, and I soon realized that Kristen had inherited not only her mother's beauty but also her sweetness and kindness. After quite a while of hugging and squealing from her mother, Kristen introduced her mom to the young man named "Bradford" that she had heard so much about over the course of the summer. I also received a hug and felt immediately welcomed.

Kristen's father, on the other hand, was not a new entity to me. Because I had an office during the internship, I also had a phone. Unbeknownst to me, Kristen had given my desk phone number to her family in case they ever needed to reach her during the workday. One day, the phone rang at my desk, and I answered it expecting to hear from one of the many law enforcement officers from whom I had requested case files. Instead, I was introduced to Kristen's father. While this should have been an uncomfortable situation, he and I ended up talking and laughing for nearly half an hour.

After that phone call, and now upon meeting him in person at his home, I realized that the man had two predominant forms of communication: jokes and sarcasm. It was a perfect fit for me. While Kristen had obviously inherited her mother's beauty, there was no doubt that she had also inherited her father's sense of humor. As I watched Kristen reunite with her family, I became aware that this girl from Michigan, with whom I had fallen so hard and so quickly in our summer at the FBI Academy, had been graced with the best attributes of both of her parents. It was therefore no great surprise to me that I also fell in love with her mom and dad. It was crystal clear to me that leaving Michigan was not going to be easy.

17

THE LAUNCH PAD

Despite the fact that Kristen's brother was getting married in just a few short days, there was no sense of panic in the household, and the big day came and went without any major problems. Being that neither Kristen nor I were adept at air travel at that point in our lives, we had not considered the exorbitant cost of flight reservations made within such a short timeframe. Fortunately, Kristen's parents allowed me to stay for an extra week so that I could get a cheaper flight. Not only was this gracious of them, but Kristen and I were thrilled to once again delay my inevitable departure for a little while longer. To make up for any inconvenience my extended stay may have caused, I decided to help out while everyone was at work. I cut the grass, which, little did I know, was firmly stepping on Kristen's mom's toes. She was very finicky about her lawn, and this was a job she took very seriously. Though a minor faux pas, I felt comfortable knowing that the mowing I provided was consistent with the high standards of the landscaping company I worked for back home.

While I was confident in my landscaping abilities, I was a little less so with my dishwashing experience. Growing up, my mother was our dishwasher. As I crept into my teen years, my mom would often coax me into drying the dishes by putting oldies cassettes into her under-cabinet radio so that we could sing while she washed and I dried. While this left me well-versed in the lyrics of the golden oldies, it also left me woefully unprepared for operating an automatic dishwasher. Still, feeling like I had to repay my stay, I decided to tackle the dirty dish backlog at Kristen's house. As I eyed the receptacle for the dishwashing fluid, I incorrectly assumed that Dawn dish soap would do the job. After all, this was what we used at our house to wash the dishes.

I filled the tiny cup with Dawn and went about my business, certain that my thoughtfulness in washing and putting away the dishes would be well-received. When I returned to the kitchen some time later, I quickly realized the error of my ways. Instead of a gently humming dishwasher, I was greeted with a kitchen full of bubbles. The scene was nearly identical to Bobby Brady's classic tackling of the laundry in Kristen's and my beloved Brady Bunch. In a panic, I searched the house for anything to wipe up the soapy bubbles that were overflowing onto the kitchen floor from the angry dishwasher. Finding some beach towels, I fought back against the wall of foam while praying that no one would come home sooner than expected to witness my idiocy in full bloom. After what seemed like an unyielding battle of the wills, the tide of the war began to turn as I slowly restored the kitchen to its original condition. My fevered efforts proved effective, and no one was the wiser. Later that evening, in a moment of honesty, I informed Kristen of my day's events. She laughed, gently educated me on my mistake, and not-so-coincidentally likened me to Bobby Brady. Yep, our compatibility was hard to ignore.

Sadly, the time had finally come for me to return to my life in the Philadelphia area. The first day of my final semester at Temple was about to begin, and it was long overdue that we both returned to a sense of normalcy. I drove Kristen's vehicle to Detroit Metro Airport with her in the passenger seat. I was getting very used to having her in that position in my life. Unfortunately, as we made our way down I-275 toward the airport, we knew the time was ticking. My impending departure marked not only the official end of the most wonderful summer of our lives but also the beginning of our future filled with constant separation at best, or an eventual breakup at worst. While we were both inherently rational and cautious by nature, we had uncharacteristically discussed marriage on multiple occasions during our three-month relationship. It seemed we had both realized that our connection was unlike any we had experienced before. Something was different about us and our relationship. With this in mind, we said goodbye to one another for the first time. I turned to board the jetway for a flight to Philadelphia while Kristen turned toward her existing life in Michigan. Unfortunately, this would not be the last time we left one another heading in different directions.

✳✳✳

My return to the Philadelphia area proved to be the start of a whirlwind of activity. A couple of weeks after getting home from Michigan, I began my final semester at Temple. Although I had been unaware of internships prior to applying to the FBI, I soon became addicted to them. After I initially applied for the FBI's internship, I traveled to the Norristown Police Department and requested a meeting with the Chief of Police. Sitting in his office, I explained my interest in law enforcement and my educational pursuits. I then asked if his department offered any internship opportunities. Sadly, he replied that they did not. Then, out of nowhere, I asked if he would be willing to start one. After some brief consideration, the Chief looked at me and said, "Sure. Why not?" This led to my being brought on as a Paid Detective Intern in their Detective Bureau. Earning a handsome salary of $5 per hour, I worked at the department several afternoons a week for about nine months, performing data entry, filing, processing prisoners, aiding in the accountability of evidence, and assisting with minor investigations. They allowed me to tag along for jail visits, drug raids, and crime scene investigations. The detectives at the Norristown Police Department were very kind and gracious to me, and I learned a very important lesson: don't be afraid to ask for what you want.

During my fall semester, I also secured an internship with the Bureau of Alcohol, Tobacco, and Firearms (ATF) in Philadelphia for college credit. This afforded me the opportunity to view federal law enforcement through the lens of a different agency. Then, during my last semester at Temple, the Criminal Justice Department held a job fair where representatives from various federal, state, and local agencies operating within the criminal justice field came to meet with students. I was excited to see that a recruiter from the FBI in Philadelphia was on site. Sitting in my suit with resumes in hand, I couldn't wait for my turn to speak with him. After all, I had just spent the summer working at the

FBI Academy, assisting profilers, and shaking hands with not only the FBI Director but also Janet Reno, the United States Attorney General. I was now certain that I wanted to be a Special Agent with the FBI. I was equally confident that this FBI agent sitting at his booth would be impressed that I had just completed the highly competitive FBI Honors Internship Program.

Apparently, I was a bit rash in my assumption. The agent could not have been less interested in me or what I had to say. He certainly wasn't interested in the fact that I had just returned from three months at Quantico. One would think this would be a great topic of discussion: "Good for you. How did you like it?" "What unit did they have you working in?" "Would you recommend the program to others?" Any of these questions would have been excellent starting points for a meaningful discussion between a so-called 'recruiter' and a young man desperately anxious to join his organization. Instead, I received a surly and generic interaction on par with being checked out by a grumpy cashier at the grocery store. In no uncertain terms, he informed me that at twenty-four years of age, I was too young to be an agent, and I would never become one without a Master's degree. His callous behavior and the information he provided left me devastated, and I felt as if I had crumbled into a small pile of dejected sawdust right in front of him.

At that moment, I realized that something was definitely different about me. Having been raised by parents who likely would have been too afraid to enter the room and would have apologized profusely for wasting the poor man's time, I should have slinked off and headed home with my tail between my legs. Maybe it was my time in the Army, my time at college, my time working around law enforcement, or any combination thereof, but my resolve solidified right then and there. My disappointment turned to anger and determination. This potato spud of a government servant was not going to tell me "No."

After visiting another booth, I watched as the agent walked to the bathroom. Completely resolved, I followed him in and took the urinal immediately to his left. As we both finished our business, I took a resume and stuck it in his general direction.

"I just wanted you to have this and to let you know that I'll be on your side of the table in five years."

My eyes burrowed into his as he took my resume. I then washed my hands and walked out. Neither of us said another word. If he was trying to deter me, he had chosen the wrong approach. I was now more committed to my dream than before.

***

That evening, Silopi sat in my lap as I told my parents what had transpired during the career fair earlier that day. My father, the eternal optimist, who was likely operating under the delusion that the recruiter would hand me a badge and gun right there at the job fair, shared my initial dejection. In contrast, my mother's underlying lack of self-confidence caused her to look at me as if I had chosen to wipe my nose on the Pope's robe. The fire to accomplish my goal of one day working for the FBI was lit, but I am not sure my parents completely comprehended my determination at that moment.

By December, I had completed my final course at Temple University. For someone who had been absolutely petrified of attending college and completely insecure about his academic abilities, I graduated summa cum laude with a 3.94 GPA. This proved to be another incredibly important life lesson for me: as long as you are willing to work hard, you should never count yourself out.

I was thrilled to have finished college and proud that my newfound degree had not cost my parents a cent. Kristen flew out for my graduation in January 1996, and with my diploma in hand, I was now focused on a two-pronged goal. First, I needed to get a job in law enforcement until I was old enough to become an agent. Second, I needed to ensure the job was in Michigan.

Day after day, I completed applications and sent resumes to nearly every police and investigative agency in the greater Detroit area. Silopi sat on the bed as I printed and packaged these documents for the mail. It became a mission. Each day, I placed letters in the mail while keeping track of my applications and correspondence in a giant accordion folder. Something had to break, given the sheer volume of documents I was mailing. I told my impatient self that God doesn't work on my schedule, but this did not necessarily assuage the impetuousness of youth. In the interim, I began working full-time for the private investigator, which had me conducting surveillance five to six days a week across the tri-state area. With no such thing as email, I hurried home each day, hoping that the mail would bring an invitation to interview for a law enforcement position in Michigan.

Instead, I received seemingly unending letters from police departments advising, "We are not hiring at the moment, but we will be sure to keep your resume on file."

Finally, I received word from a department approximately thirty minutes from Kristen's home that expressed interest in me. I flew to Detroit, participated in their required testing, and then sat down for a meeting with their Chief. I felt good. I felt confident. This was going to happen. I was going to become a law enforcement officer, and better yet, it would be in Michigan. The thought of working in my desired profession so close to where my girlfriend lived excited me beyond words. My confidence grew as I sat and chatted with the Chief. He complimented me on my education. That was a great sign. He complimented me on my GPA. Another great sign. He complimented me on my internships with the Norristown Police Department, the ATF, and the FBI. Clearly, this was going to be a shoo-in.

Then, after all of the Chief's compliments, he looked at me and continued, "But I can't hire you."

I'm not sure if my jaw dropped, but there is a distinct possibility that it hit the top of my dress shoes right in front of the Chief. "Can I ask why, sir?"

"Because you are going to leave us for the FBI. We'll spend money putting you through the academy and training you, and then you will leave us after a couple of years to join the FBI."

It was hard to put up any meaningful defense to his prophetic observation. I am not exactly sure what he saw in my background, but he hit the nail on the head. He wished me luck, and I thanked him for his time. As I walked out of the building, I felt conflicted. I was so hopeful that this was my path, and it felt like a huge disappointment to come so close and have the rug pulled out from under me. On the other hand, Garth Brooks sang about thanking God for unanswered prayers just six years earlier. Part of me couldn't help but think that the Chief had just done me a favor. Shortly thereafter, my true path began to shine just a tad brighter.

I learned that the FBI was looking to hire for a position called the Investigative Specialist. Though not an agent position, Investigative Specialists were part of a Special Surveillance Group (SSG) trained in conducting physical surveillance to assist in National Security investigations. Essentially, they followed and monitored the activities of suspected spies and terrorists. Since I was already conducting surveillance daily at the private investigation firm, this seemed like a natural fit for me. Moreover, such a position might serve as a stepping stone to becoming a Special Agent. With the premise that I could always decline the offer, I threw my hat into the ring. My application soon led to an interview. Things were not panning out on the Michigan job front, and I had slowly come to the realization that I might need to take another approach. Then, during a trip to Michigan, God's plan became much clearer.

While on the campus of Kristen's university, my pager went off. Though clearly a technology of the distant past, the pager was still an effective means of communication. Removing it from my belt, I noticed a number with a "703" area code. Having spent the previous summer at the FBI Academy, I immediately recognized the number as originating in Northern Virginia. I became excited—maybe this was related to my FBI application. Finding an available desk phone in the lobby, I called the number displayed on my pager.

My suspicions were quickly confirmed when my call was answered by a Supervisory Investigative Specialist. After identifying myself, the supervisor delivered incredible news: I had been selected to become an Investigative Specialist. I could hardly contain my excitement; I had just been offered a position in the organization I so desperately wanted to join. Unfortunately, this also opened a whole new set of logistical challenges for my relationship with Kristen. It is amazing how much can go through your mind in such a brief period of time. If I took the job, where would I be stationed? Should I pass up an opportunity to work with the FBI for a relationship that had not progressed beyond long-distance dating? These questions ricocheted around my mind before the supervisor's voice interrupted.

"Are you interested?" he asked.

I had to make a choice. Sometimes, when you have too many balls in the air, it helps to put at least one of them down on the table.

"Yes, sir," I answered enthusiastically. Then came one of the worst questions I have ever been asked: "How does New York sound?"

Ugh. Just a few weeks earlier, I had conducted surveillance on a worker's compensation claim in New York City. When I had to move my vehicle to get a better look at the subject's front door, it literally took me half an hour to go around the block. The thought of staying on the East Coast in an even more congested area, after having tasted the sweet openness of the Midwest, felt like that old grainy slow-motion video of the circus freak taking a cannonball shot off his stomach.

Kristen's father had often jokingly likened these types of decisions to seeing your mother-in-law going over a cliff in your brand-new Cadillac. It was a situation that brought both glee and dread at the same time.

Then, not unlike when I asked the Chief at the Norristown Police Department if he'd be willing to start an internship program for me, I blurted out what would eventually prove to be the second most important question of my life: "How about Detroit?" I asked.

There was a slight hesitation on the other end of the connection before the supervisor asked a clarifying question of his own. "You want to go to Detroit?" he asked, sounding incredulous. Apparently, for this gentleman, the Motor City paled in comparison to the Big Apple.

"If you have any openings there," I clarified. I was again met with a brief hesitation. I could not quite figure out the reasons for the man's delays in addressing my inquiries.

"I'll call you back in ten minutes," the supervisor said before quickly hanging up the phone.

Hearing only one side of the conversation, I updated Kristen on the call, my offer, and the looming assignment to New York City. It was a classic Catch-22 situation. Employment with the FBI was a dream come true, but being assigned to New York City... well, that was far less desirable. I began to ponder what was happening in Northern Virginia at that moment and why the man had hung up on me so quickly. What did it mean? Had I just shot myself in the foot? Had I already demonstrated a sense of insubordination by asking for an alternative assignment from an organization I did not even work for yet? Though I didn't start the timer on my watch when I hung up the phone, the ten-minute timeframe seemed to stretch on for hours as I repeatedly checked my pager for a callback number. Then, finally, the little black plastic box buzzed to life in my hand. I quickly dialed the same number as before, and the same man answered. His statement was straight and to the point.

"We are just opening a new SSG office in Detroit. If you want to go to Detroit, you would be the first person assigned there."

Things seemed to move in slow motion as I took in his words. I could not believe what I had just been told. Not only was I being given a chance to work with the FBI, but I was also being offered an opportunity to work in Detroit. In an unexpected phone call, I had just been offered my dream agency in my ideal location. The months of letter after letter and disappointment after disappointment dissolved in an instant. Again, the voice on the other end of the line shocked me back into coherence.

"Do you want it?" the supervisor asked.

"Yes, sir. Absolutely," I exclaimed. I did not even try to hide my enthusiasm at that point.

"Okay. Great," he replied. "I will put your orders together and we'll get back to you with a class date."

"Thank you so much," I said. "I'm looking forward to it."

Hanging up the phone, Kristen and I were both in a state of shock. Especially for me, a proud defensive pessimist, this alignment of the planets was unexpected. Despite my surging joy, this news also brought a number of concerns. Yes, I would be working with the FBI, which put me one step closer to hopefully becoming an agent. And yes, getting a job in the Detroit area would allow my relationship with Kristen to progress normally, rather than through a six-hundred-mile separation with periodic visits. However, this news also meant that I would be moving to another state for a girl, or at least partially for a girl. This reality naturally placed a lot of pressure on both Kristen and me, as well as our relationship. Just as concerning was the fact that the guy who had been so homesick a handful of years earlier would be moving away from his family yet again. Would this time be any different? Lastly, my move meant that Silopi would also be forced to leave the home she had known for nearly all her life. How would she take such a move? In my initial excitement, I failed to realize that my impending steps forward would severely impact both Silopi and my parents. It felt like this next phase of my life was just reaching the launch pad. Unfortunately, my excitement was also accompanied by a fair amount of worry and concern over the ones I loved.

18

THE END & THE BEGINNING

My parents could not have been prouder that I had been selected to work full-time with the Federal Bureau of Investigation. Thankfully, they were also extremely supportive of my move to the Detroit area for this new job. I shared my feelings of guilt about leaving with my mother. I was incredibly excited to be starting a career with the greatest law enforcement agency in the world and thrilled to finally be residing in the same state as Kristen. Still, I had a wonderful relationship with both of my parents, and I knew that leaving would be hard for them... again. When I discussed these concerns with my mother, she would not hear of it. She was happy and proud of me, and that overshadowed any sadness she might feel about my departure. My mother then offered me an incredible and much-appreciated piece of wisdom: "Closeness does not mean proximity." In other words, we didn't have to live in the same house, or even in the same state, to maintain a close relationship. Her words were both simple and profound, instantly making me feel better about leaving.

However, the remainder of our conversation was not quite as selfless.

"What are you going to do with Silopi?" she asked.

This had not even crossed my mind. Of course, Silopi was coming to Michigan with me. As I conveyed this to my mother, she quickly countered with an argument that she had obviously, though secretly, considered. Was it fair to move Silopi six hundred miles away? She had been living in our home for nearly five years at that point. Berlin and Turkey were part of her distant memory. Would she become confused by the move? If I was going to be working all day, that meant Silopi would be alone all day. Was that fair to her?

As my mother strategically laid out her rhetorical questions, it became crystal clear. The woman who never allowed us to have a pet larger than a hamster and who recommended that Silopi live in our cold, unfinished basement had obviously fallen in love with the tiny cat I had brought home from the Army. It was impossible to ignore that the feeling was mutual. It was not uncommon to find Silopi lying with my mom on the couch in the evenings or sitting on my dad's lap as he read the newspaper. If she was my feline daughter, then she was also my parents' feline granddaughter. Through her litany of rhetorical questions, my mother drove her point home: she was not willing to lose both Silopi and me in my move to Michigan. As was often the case in discussions with my mother over the years, her view on the subject seemed to be the correct one.

I once heard it said that dogs bond to people, but cats bond to locations. This was Silopi's home. More importantly, between working long and odd hours with the private investigator and my frequent trips to Michigan, I was spending less and less time at home. My assumption that she would make the move with me from the East Coast to the Midwest was beginning to feel more like a selfish decision than a rational plan. During the internship the previous summer, I had spent nearly three months away from Silopi. Now, during the summer of 1996, I had just spent another five weeks away from her at the FBI Academy, learning how to properly conduct surveillance. The writing on the wall was unmistakable: the rest of my life was about to begin. Although my journey would start in Michigan, where it would take me was anyone's guess. It just didn't seem fair to drag Silopi along with me as I tried to figure it all out.

So, I loaded up my Norristown life into my Jeep Cherokee and a pickup truck that my dad had borrowed from work. Saying goodbye to Silopi was harder than I would have thought. She had been there every step of the way as I transitioned from military life to civilian life to college life, and now to my law enforcement life. Just as I had been a sense of security for her as we moved from Southwest Asia to Germany to the greater Philadelphia area, she had also become a source of security for me. At a time of seemingly incessant change and uncertainty, she remained a constant. And now, almost exactly five years after we met in the heat and dust of her namesake town, I was leaving her for good. This realization brought with it a profound sadness, which proved to be an unavoidable counterweight to the immense excitement I felt about starting a career with the FBI and moving to Michigan to be near Kristen.

With the vehicles packed for my move the following morning, I went to bed for the last official time in Norristown. As she had done every night since I returned home from the Army, Silopi followed me up the steps and jumped on the bed. On this night, however, she did not immediately curl up between my legs over the covers, nor did she bat at the blankets to slink under the sheets. Instead, she perched herself on my chest as I lay on my back in the darkness. Nearly nose to nose, she sat looking at me as I stroked her back. Animals are intuitive, and she obviously knew things were changing.

A couple of years earlier, my mom had slipped at the small delicatessen down the street where she worked part-time. In trying to brace herself, she broke her arm. As if this were not bad enough, she also developed a rare swelling disorder that exacerbated her pain and extended her recovery time. She recounted instances in which her pain became so overwhelming that she would sit on the end of her bed and cry. During those times, Silopi would appear from nowhere like a highly trained rescue animal and sit by her side. My mom always felt as if Silopi was telling her, "I know. It's okay." My mom would then sit and cry, petting Silopi and soaking in the comfort that the little black-and-white cat's presence brought.

Lying there on my last night in Norristown, Silopi was obviously feeling the same sadness from me. As she purred on my chest, I swear I could hear those same words from her: "I know. It's okay." We both fell asleep in that position.

***

In life, a key component to happiness is knowing who you are and understanding your own flaws and weaknesses. One of mine is the innate tendency to push things. I tend to exist in a state somewhere between motivation and impatience. If I am being completely honest, sometimes that needle pushes much closer to the impatience point of the spectrum than I would prefer. I certainly felt this way as I waited at the Reception Station at Fort Benning, anxious to get Basic Training started. In many ways, it is an inherited family trait; my mother often chose speed over precision. This left her forever searching for items she misplaced in her haste to complete a task. If our family crest had a subheading, it would read: "It's better to do the wrong thing quickly than to take your time and do it right."

This familial propensity woke me from my sleep shortly after Silopi and I had dozed off. The lights went on in my head, and I was ready to go. As Kristen had experienced during that first Christmas with my family, cleanup efforts began immediately after the last package was opened; the party was over. My new life in Michigan was about to start in just a few hours, but I couldn't wait. Despite it being shortly after midnight, I was eager to literally get the show on the road. I dressed and headed downstairs, wide awake and ready for the nine-hour drive to Michigan. Silopi followed me down as I found my mom dozing on the couch, having fallen asleep to the late-night shows.

I explained to her that I was awake and wanted to start the drive. She was clearly the source of our family's underlying impatience, as she did not even question my decision to leave at such an ungodly hour. I hugged her goodbye and promised to drive safely. She agreed to do the same, as she and my dad would be leaving in the morning to bring the rest of my things and help get my new apartment squared away.

Silopi followed me to the back door. I scooped her up in my arms, as I had done so many times before. I held her for a moment, trying not to dwell too deeply on the significance of this particular departure. Placing her back on the floor, I walked out of the house I had grown up in. It would be the last time I had a Norristown address.

Making my way down the walkway toward my awaiting vehicle, I stopped to take a final look at my home. As I did, I saw a little black silhouette appear in the window next to the back door. A radiator was positioned just under the window, and my mom had taken to placing a folded rug on top of it so that Silopi could nap in warmth and watch the world outside. Now, as she sat on the radiator, I could see her little outline sitting motionless as she observed me leaving. In life, turning a page is always difficult. The turning of this page was even more challenging because of the little black-and-white bookmark now sitting in the window, marking a chapter of my life I had just finished. My headlights illuminated her as I backed out of my parking space.

"Bye-bye, 'Soapy,'" I said under my breath.

Putting my Cherokee into drive, I made my way to the turnpike that would carry me away from Norristown and toward the start of my new and uncharted life in Michigan.

19

I'VE LOVED THESE DAYS

For someone who had been so homesick in the Army, it is curious that my drive away from Norristown on that early morning in September of 1996 would mark the fact that I never lived in Pennsylvania again. For two years, I lived and worked with the FBI in Michigan. I set up residence in a little apartment that Kristen and her mom had found for me prior to my move. Despite our mutual fears about my relocating to the area, my relationship with Kristen blossomed. We were together constantly, and her parents became like my own family.

My dream of becoming an FBI agent came true two years later, and contrary to the negative prognostications of the recruiter in Philadelphia, I not only started the sixteen-week New Agents Training at the age of twenty-six, but I did so without a Master's degree. It was yet another reminder that you should never allow the naysayers in your life to dissuade you from your dreams.

During New Agents Training, my class was assigned a tactical instructor who introduced himself to us and explained that he had grown up in a small coal mining town in western Pennsylvania.

After class, I introduced myself and mentioned that my mother had also grown up in a small coal mining town in Pennsylvania.

"Where did you grow up?" I asked.

"Oh, it's a small town of only four hundred people; you wouldn't have heard of it," he replied.

"What was the name?" I asked again.

"Trust me," he said. "You wouldn't have heard of it."

At my insistence, he finally divulged the name of his hometown: "Jerome."

I immediately began to laugh. "My mother is from Jerome," I said. We were both shocked at the coincidence that an FBI agent and a new agent in training both had ties to a four-hundred-person town in Somerset County, Pennsylvania. Having previously visited Jerome for family reunions and having heard so many stories of my mother's upbringing, we discussed the people and places in that tiny area.

Then, with a sense of pride and wonder, he announced to me, "You know we have sewers now."

In a sign of small-town solidarity, I applauded the modern, albeit long-overdue, advancement of a sewage system and then recounted the story of how my mother's sister had gotten sick as a child after falling into the town's previous sewage system, known as the 'stink ditch'. Again, it seemed that God had inserted a tiny Easter egg into my New Agents Training. I could hardly wait to tell my mom.

***

I equated my training at the FBI Academy to a cross between Army Basic Training and college. Though stressful, it proved to be more than manageable. As one of the instructors explained on the first day of training, the FBI had already spent a great deal of money just getting us to the Academy. As such, they actually wanted us to succeed. That announcement definitely took the edge off for me. Where things seemed much more like Basic Training than college was the day each of us was required to experience the effects of pepper spray.

As we stood in a line, instructors came by and sprayed the oleoresin capsicum (OC) spray directly into our eyes and nose. We then distanced ourselves from the instructor with a shove and simulated drawing our sidearm with one hand while holding our eye open with the other. OC spray is designed to burn the eyes, cause temporary blindness, induce coughing, and irritate the throat and nasal cavity. As I stood there retching with my nose running down to my ankles, I was immediately reminded of the day of unending gas attacks at Fort Benning. I wondered what masochistic gene I must have been born with to once again put myself in a position of having federal officials do this type of thing to me on purpose. There had to be other career choices.

Similar to Basic Training, another key source of stress during New Agents Training was learning where you would be assigned for your first duty station. This was certainly the case for me. The rule at that time was that nobody returned to the office in which they in-processed. Since I had in-processed through the Detroit Field Office, that meant there was no way I would be returning. Secretly, I hoped that the Bureau would readily grant the wishes of someone who actually wanted to be assigned to Detroit. However, I hung my misguided hopes on the possibility that if I did not receive orders to Detroit, at least I would be assigned to the Philadelphia Office so I could be back with my family.

Earlier in the training, we were directed to rank our preferences from 1 to 56 for which field office we would each like to be assigned. I placed Detroit at the top of my list, hoping that its low desirability would play in my favor. After all, I wasn't asking to be transferred to Tampa or Honolulu. I then placed Philadelphia as my second choice. While it was not as desirable for me personally, at least I'd be home.

When we finally received our assignment letters, I was disheartened to learn that my rationale was way off base. I received my twenty-sixth choice: Newark, New Jersey. Interestingly, the young lady who sat behind me throughout the training received Philadelphia as her assignment; it was her twentieth choice. I realized at that moment, when it comes to a monstrous bureaucracy like the FBI, someone must have thought, "Why make one person happy when you can make two people unhappy?"

Yet again, God cracked a window for me after slamming a door in my face. I had learned through the grapevine that they were looking to assign a new agent from our class to the Atlantic City office out of the Newark Division. I also discovered that one of the agents from the Atlantic City office was at the Academy on temporary duty. Determined to make lemonade out of the handful of lemons I had received in my assignment letter, I located the Atlantic City agent and asked to meet with him in the cafeteria. My plan was to make a good impression on him in hopes that he would report back to his office that I would be a valuable addition to their tiny office of twenty-five agents.

My gamble paid off. A couple of weeks later, my orders were amended. Instead of being assigned to Newark Division Headquarters, I would be assigned to the Atlantic City Resident Agency. The transfer took me away from Kristen yet again, but at least I was a mere hour and a half from home. More importantly, I was now working in and around the shore towns where I had grown up vacationing with my family. It was the best possible outcome of a less-than-desirable situation.

***

The transfer threw me headfirst into my dream job. Unfortunately, it also thrust Kristen and me back into the world of long-distance dating. She looked for employment in South Jersey while visiting me. Sadly, in the Atlantic City area, it seemed that the only available job openings were for law enforcement officers, blackjack dealers, and bank robbers. None of these options seemed to pique Kristen's interest.

Both of our careers were in full swing, but we continued to keep an eye out for an opportunity to bring us back to the same state. Then, out of the blue, a posting crossed my desk. The FBI was looking for an agent with a counterintelligence background for a transfer to the Detroit Division. I couldn't believe it. It looked as if things were lining up again. I had worked as an Investigative Specialist in the Detroit Office for two years, doing surveillance for the very same agents on the very same squad to which the Bureau was looking to transfer someone. What were the chances?

I immediately wrote a communication expressing my interest in the transfer.On the day the posting closed and all applications were to be submitted, I called the Transfer Unit at FBI Headquarters to inquire about the number of people who had requested the transfer. I wanted to know what my chances were.

"Hi. Can you tell me how many people applied for the counterintelligence transfer to Detroit?" I asked the woman in the Transfer Unit.

"Including you?" she replied.

"Yes," I smiled. "Including me."

After a quick calculation, she gave me the news. "One," she said.

"What?" I asked incredulously. It sounded as if she was telling me that out of an organization of nearly eleven thousand agents, I was the only one who had applied for the transfer. My suspicions were quickly confirmed.

"Yep. You are the only one who put in for it."

I couldn't believe it. Lightning had struck again. I was going to be transferred back to Detroit. I quickly called Kristen to inform her of the news. Like me, her excitement came through the phone.

I returned to my work with my head spinning. Should I look for vacancies in the same apartment complex I had just moved out of a little more than a year ago? Was that too far of a drive to Detroit each morning? I had so many questions.

Approximately forty-five minutes later, my hopes and questions were dashed against the jagged rocks of bureaucracy. Another woman from FBI Headquarters called me back to gently break the news.

"You're not going anywhere," she said.

"I'm sorry?" I said, looking for clarification.

"You're not even finished with your probationary period. They are not going to transfer you if you are still on probation."

As a new agent, it was necessary to complete a two-year probationary period during which you were required to complete a variety of experiences, such as testifying, conducting a search warrant, writing an arrest warrant, etc. Being that I was lucky enough to be assigned to a small but extremely busy office like Atlantic City, I had completed all of these requirements months earlier. Moreover, I was only a handful of months away from completing my probationary period. But such is life in a bureaucracy.

Still, I wanted additional clarity about this logic. Truth be told, what I actually wanted to do was pick at the scab that had already started to form during the course of the phone call.

"Just to clarify," I began. "The FBI would rather have nobody than me?"

"That's correct," she curtly replied.

I decided to poke the bear a little more in an attempt to make the woman understand the inherent flaws underlying this organizational logic. "What you are telling me is that you would rather hang a suit coat over the back of an empty chair than have me fill that empty position?" I asked.

"That's what I'm telling you," she stated with her unique and consistent sense of callousness.

"Okay. Thanks," I said, hanging up the phone.

I learned two things from this exchange: a) I was nothing more than a drone in a monstrous bureaucratic beehive; and b) it is physically possible to place second in a one-man race.

***

Living and working along the South Jersey shore, only ninety minutes from my parents, allowed me to see them and Silopi fairly frequently as my work schedule and travel to Michigan permitted. But during these visits, it became clear that something had changed. Silopi would come running to greet me as usual, but her decision to sleep with me or my parents had become a coin toss. Because of my distance, she had become my parents' cat. It was both inevitable and understandable. It was sad to see this sweet little part of my life fade away, but I was also happy that my parents had Silopi.

Four of their five children were now out of the house, and the oldest three already had children of their own. My younger brother, though still living at home, was busy with his own life and always seemed to be out. As such, Silopi became the little creature to whom my parents could now cast their love and care. When I called home or visited, I would hear stories about what Silopi was up to or the funny things she had done. In the evenings, she would follow my father to bed or sleep with my mom on the couch while she watched television. Where she used to bat at my blankets to get underneath, she now did the same with my parents.

"I don't know how she can breathe under there," my mom would exclaim every time she told me about it.

Silopi seemed to have developed a strong attachment to my father and would often follow him around the house, batting at his heels as he walked or trailing behind him, chirping all the way. Whenever he entered the house, he would call out her name, and she would come running. Around dinner time each evening, Silopi would greet my father at the door and then pace around her food bowl while he went upstairs to change out of his work clothes. Back and forth she would pace and chirp at my mother as she placed dinner on the table.

'Beep... B-Beep... B-Beep... Beep.'

Silopi always made her point clear to my mother: 'Where is he? I'm hungry. Does he have to take so long getting changed? Can't you tell him to hurry?'

She would continue to pace around her food until my father finally sat down at the table. Once he did, she would begin to eat her own meal. My mom was never quite certain why Silopi felt she had to wait for the two of them to sit down before she started to eat. I guess I must have unwittingly raised her with good table manners.

While Silopi and my father became close buddies, she also became an annoyance to him whenever he tried to read the newspaper. Routinely, as he engaged in this nightly ritual, she would jump onto his lap as if she were reading the story below the fold while he was reading the one above. The problem arose when she was no longer getting the attention she felt she deserved; then she would start batting at the newspaper, making it impossible for my father to read. My dad would place her on the floor and try to shoo her away. Undoubtedly, Silopi would return to his lap a short while later to repeat the dance all over again. It drove my father batty, though admittedly, it was not really that far of a drive.

One evening, while my mother was in the bathroom preparing for bed, she received a visit from Silopi. As she opened a jar of Noxzema, Silopi tore out of the bathroom in a black-and-white streak. My mom concluded that Silopi did not like the menthol smell of the Noxzema skin cream. Always thinking, my mother soon realized that she had unexpectedly found a solution for my father's newspaper problem. From that point forward, when my dad's newspaper came out, so too did the Noxzema jar. He would simply remove the lid, place the open jar by his chair, and POOF... no more Silopi. Who would have thought that a little jar of Noxzema could cure a growing case of too much togetherness?

***

Looking back on my first assignment as an FBI Special Agent, Atlantic City proved to be a great place to start my career. Unfortunately, it did not allow Kristen and me to start an actual life together. We were in a state of limbo, and something had to give. Like most people, I found that when putting a puzzle together, the first order of business was to assemble the border to see where the rest of the pieces would fall into place. The edge pieces help define the rest of the picture. So, on a trip to Michigan that spring, I asked Kristen's dad to lunch. We had a close relationship, so the invitation did not seem unusual. However, I had ulterior motives for the meal. I was secretly looking to put the edge pieces of my life together. As such, I asked for his daughter's hand in marriage—a nerve-wracking question for any young man. His answer to my unexpected inquiry was mercifully quick.

"Sure," he said.

Unbeknownst to me, he had a question of his own: "Are you going to eat the rest of those fries?"

In typical fashion for Kristen's father, I received permission to marry his daughter for a simple dowry of a half-serving of French fries. I couldn't help but walk away from the exchange feeling like I got the better end of the deal. Now, I can't speak on behalf of my soon-to-be father-in-law... the man really liked French fries.

I shocked Kristen with my proposal later that day, and after a forty-five-minute "job interview" in which I thoroughly outlined the importance of putting first things first, she agreed to marry me. We initially planned to marry in September of 2000. However, shortly after our engagement, Kristen received word that she had been hired by the FBI for a job just outside the FBI Academy. This meant that we could apply for a No-Cost Common Household Transfer. In other words, I could request to follow Kristen to Virginia as long as I paid the transfer costs. In addition to being an exciting new career for her, this opportunity promised that we would be in the same state together as a married couple—a situation that most newly married couples take for granted. Unfortunately, the Bureau would not grant the transfer until we were married. As such, we bumped up our wedding by ten months and got married in November 1999. In an unconventional move, my best man was my father—the man who was always there for me.

Despite living in the Atlantic City area for two years, I was not a gambler. My experiences with the FBI were a prime reason I steered clear of this particular vice. Kristen got caught in a six-month hiring freeze, which meant that we wouldn't have had to move the wedding up anyway. So, instead of immediately combining our belongings into a new marital home after our honeymoon, I returned to Atlantic City while Kristen went back to her bedroom in her parents' house. It was yet another separation that we were forced to wait out.

Months later, Kristen was hired, and my transfer was granted. I requested a transfer to the Richmond Division but received orders to the Washington Field Office in Washington, D.C., instead. I asked to be assigned to a criminal squad, but they thought it would be better for me to work on a National Security squad. Sadly, beggars can't be choosers, and I was just glad to finally be living with my new bride.

***

In April 2000, five months after our marriage, Kristen drove out from Michigan while I drove down from South Jersey to our new apartment in Northern Virginia. Both sets of parents helped with the move, and we started our new jobs with the FBI a few days later.

We quickly transitioned to the hectic pace of the DC area. Each morning, I drove north into the city while Kristen drove south toward Quantico. We now lived just minutes from the apartment complex where we were housed during our internship five years earlier. Being back in the area where we met was exciting, and the fact that both of us were now working for the Bureau was even more thrilling. However, returning to our roots after nearly five years of seemingly incessant logistical separations—there is no word to describe that feeling.

Living just a stone's throw from the nation's capital made us feel like we were in the heart of the action, but it also made us feel like one of thousands of tiny fish swimming around the vast federal government reef that connected us all. Nearly everyone worked for the same mothership. We all wore suits, military uniforms, or some form of professional attire. Women in skirts wore sneakers as they raced from the nearest Metro station to their respective offices. From there, they would swap out their sneakers for heels, only to reverse the process for their evening commutes home. At times, it seemed like the only thing that differentiated one governmental drone from another was the varying security badges attached to the lanyards hanging around our necks.

Traffic was all-encompassing in the DC area. Drivers from every corner of the globe traversed the highways, bringing their own unique driving habits and abilities. The result of this vehicular melting pot was unending gridlock. Residents made every attempt to counteract the highway congestion that proved to be the colossal headache we all shared. Some, including myself, would wake up at three or four in the morning to beat the traffic into the city. Those living further south in Virginia might drive to the train station, catch the train, and then take the Metro to an area close to their office. From there, they would walk the rest of the way.

For me, attempting to beat traffic meant packing my work clothes in my government car the night before so that I could roll right out of bed, put on workout clothes, and head to the gym at the Washington Field Office. My rationale was that exercising and showering at work would save me valuable time that could be spent on my commute. As a result, each morning in the locker room, I said a silent prayer that I hadn't forgotten to pack clean socks or underwear the night before.

Perhaps the most interesting anti-traffic solution was the Slug line. In what can only be considered sanctioned hitchhiking, commuters would meet at various locations throughout the area and wait in line according to their final destination. People looking for a ride to the Pentagon would stand in one line, while commuters heading to Judiciary Square or the Navy Yard would wait in another. Then, a random motorist would pull up to the line that matched their final destination and pick up three strangers to ride along with them to work. It was a completely symbiotic relationship: the three strangers got a ride to work, while the driver gained the requisite number of occupants needed to use the High Occupancy Vehicle (HOV) lanes, which promised slightly less traffic and a potentially quicker ride to work. You could always tell which cars were carrying slug riders because they tended to have the most eclectic mix of passengers. A car would pass by, driven by a young woman in her twenties wearing a business suit. Her passengers might include a military officer in uniform, a sixty-year-old Black woman in business casual attire, and a young man with a beard, a man-bun, and a flannel shirt. It wasn't just the varied ages, ethnicities, and clothing that identified them as slug line passengers; it was also the fact that they all wore headphones, ensuring that no one would be forced to speak to a stranger during their hopefully not-so-long commute. It was a completely grassroots arrangement that functioned without any government interference or official regulation. More importantly, it demonstrated how far people were willing to go to minimize commute times in the DC area.

***

Kristen and I had quickly settled into our new lives in Northern Virginia. Together, we were earning good money, and our jobs felt meaningful. When work ended or the weekend finally arrived, just being together was enough. That's what years of separation can do for you. We didn't need to go out; we simply appreciated each other's company. This was precisely how one particular weekend was beginning to unfold in the early fall of 2000 when our house phone rang.

It was my mother calling. Since it was a weekend morning, the call didn't seem unusual. We often called to check in on each other. However, when I answered the phone that Saturday morning, something was different in my mom's tone. Instantly, I sensed that something was wrong.

"What's wrong?" I asked.

Her hesitation and the slight quiver in her voice confirmed my initial assessment.

"Silopi died last night," she said. Her statement hung between us for a moment.

"Oh no." The shock of what I had just been told left me searching for any meaningful reply. My mom then explained what had happened.

The previous day, Silopi hadn't seemed like herself. There were times when she would walk through the house and just stop mid-motion, as if her body had been paused for a moment or two. Given that she often slept in various nooks and crannies around the house, it was hard to identify any major health concern. That night, instead of joining my parents on the bed, Silopi curled up in the armchair in their bedroom. My parents assumed that she would join them on the bed at some point during the evening, as was her usual routine.

An hour or so after they had called it a night, they were awakened by Silopi making a noise they had never heard before. It wasn't a "meow" or her usual Turkish chirping; instead, it was a panicked screech. The sound terrified my parents, and they both leapt from the bed and made their way to the chair. My mom quickly grabbed the phone and a phone book to locate an all-night veterinarian. My father wrapped Silopi in a blanket and held her as her guttural noises continued.

Laying Silopi on the bed, my dad quickly got dressed while my mom contacted a vet who told her to bring Silopi in right away. My younger brother, just coming in from a night out with friends, ran into my dad as he exited the house, holding Silopi in his arms. After hearing my dad's brief explanation of what was going on, my brother took Silopi from him, and they both entered my dad's car. Only later did my brother tell my mother that he knew Silopi had already passed when he jumped into the passenger's seat. He just couldn't bear to disclose the sad news to my father.

At the vet, my dad handed over Silopi in her blanket, unaware of my brother's suspicions. A few minutes later, the vet came out to the waiting room to let my dad know that Silopi was gone. My father was always soft-hearted. He was the type of man who would get choked up at a television commercial or when Mickey died in *Rocky III*. He would become emotional not only when one of his kids had their hearts broken by a girlfriend or boyfriend but also when they broke someone else's heart. He was a man of kindness and empathy, and Silopi's passing hit him hard—not only because she was the family's pet but because she was one of God's little creatures.

"Can I see her?" my dad asked the vet.

Per his request, my father was shown to the examination room where Silopi lay motionless. There would be no more batting at his heels or tormenting him as he tried to read the newspaper. My mom's Noxzema jar would remain in the bathroom from this point forward. In the days and weeks that followed, my dad would repeatedly tell my mother, "We are going to have to move." Every time he entered the house, he instinctively took up his goalie position, trying to keep a little black-and-white cat who was no longer there from bolting out the door. Walking through the door, his muscle memory made him want to call for her, knowing full well that she would no longer be there to respond. Everything in the house became a reminder that Silopi was no longer a part of their lives. As a simple man, his solution was to move to a new home as a means of distancing himself from the little reminders that would break his heart over and over again.

But at that moment, as he sat in the quiet examination room in the middle of the night, all he could do was stroke Silopi's black-and-white coat... and cry.

***

As my mom informed me of Silopi's passing over the phone, I stood in the bedroom of our small apartment, staring out the window. After pushing the button on the cordless phone to end the call, Kristen approached me and began rubbing my back. She had heard enough of my side of the conversation to grasp what had transpired.

"I'm sorry," she said softly.

Similar to my father, it was now my turn to cry. Yes, Silopi was just a cat. She was just a pet. As a former infantryman and now an FBI agent, one might think that the passing of a cat did not warrant tears from a grown man. However, as I stood there in our one-bedroom apartment in Northern Virginia, Silopi had not been a part of my daily life for nearly four years. Still, I could not help but reflect on how far we had come together—from her little furry body sitting in my hat in a chow tent in Turkey to sitting on the radiator and watching me through the darkness as I embarked on my new life. She was more than a pet or a companion; she was a constant at a time in my life when nothing else seemed to be. There were moves between countries, transitions from military life to civilian life to college life, and hunts for internships and law enforcement jobs. She was there for every bit of it.

Knowing she was gone made me sad. However, the sorrow was not just for her loss, but also for what she represented. My mom lobbied to keep Silopi in their home when I moved to Michigan. While her rationalizations made sense at the time, I have since come to realize that keeping Silopi was my mom's way of holding on to a piece of me. Little did I know, until I received the sad news from my mom just minutes earlier, that in many ways, Silopi was also my conduit to my parents, my family, my life in Norristown, and my young adulthood. Her passing felt like the breaking of one of the few remaining threads that connected me to my earlier life.

Then the feelings of guilt crept in. I found her. I took care of her. I brought her home. And then, I moved on with my life without her. I left her behind. Should I have vetoed my mother's ideas and just taken Silopi with me when I left? Did I abdicate my responsibilities by leaving her behind? Did she feel abandoned? These were the thoughts running through my head when I asked Kristen a simple question: "Do you think she knew I loved her?"

Considering my question, Kristen gave me a sympathetic smile, rubbed my back, and rested her head on my shoulder. "Aw, she knew," Kristen said. "You gave her a better life than she could have ever expected."

Her words made me smile through my tears.

Standing there with my dream wife and my dream career, I realized that, like my little black-and-white Turkish refugee cat, I too had received a far better life than I ever could have expected.

I then kissed my wife and gave her a little squeeze before returning to our day.

***

Looking back on it, I cannot remember much of my telephone conversation with my mom when she informed me of Silopi's passing. I remember talking about what a good girl she was and reminiscing about how I found her and the funny things she used to do. I also remember my mother telling me that the veterinarian had cut off a few of Silopi's whiskers and put them in an envelope for us to remember her. That Christmas, I received a gift from my parents that rivaled the Lutheran medal they had given me the Christmas before I joined the Army. It was a framed picture of Silopi. In the corner, pressed between the picture and the frame, were her little white whiskers. I stared at the meaningful gift and the little black-and-white face that stared back at me from behind the glass. And, like my father had done months earlier on the sad night he received Silopi's whiskers, I cried.

The years that followed that Christmas brought Kristen and me a new home, two beautiful sons, and a wonderful marriage filled with love and laughter. We traveled, we vacationed, and though ever-conscious of our finances, we have never worried for a minute about money. That was a promise to myself that I am glad and fortunate to say I kept.

Now, living once again in Michigan, I am equally proud to say that not only have my sons grown into strong and responsible young men, but they are also rabid Philadelphia Eagles and Phillies fans. While I would like to share credit with Kristen for the first part, I claim sole responsibility for the second.

Like the many soldiers I met in my brief time in the military, I will forever remain proud of where I came from. And, despite the love-hate relationship I once harbored for the U.S. Army, I am eternally grateful for the opportunity to have served our nation in this capacity. Thankfully, there have been, and continue to be, countless others who share the joy of service in keeping our country safe. Looking back on my term of service as I write this story, it is clear that I drastically changed the life of a little furball I found in the dry, dusty landscape of southeastern Turkey. I also realize that, in many ways, she changed my life as well. Finding her taught me about responsibility and the value of focusing on something beyond yourself. Her presence in my life served as a reminder that love can come from the most unexpected places if we just take the time to look around and listen.

I have told Silopi's story to many people over the years, but I told it to no one more important than Kristen. She has often said that Silopi's story is one of the things that made her fall in love with me. In light of this admission, Silopi actually changed my life as much as I changed hers. As I continue on with my life, I am aware of the role that God has played in all of it, and I am confident in His plan for Kristen and me. After all, He was the one who brought us together

… just like Silopi and me.

AFTERWORD

As you have probably realized by this point, mine is not a war story. I was not a Navy SEAL or a Green Beret. I did not storm a machine gun nest or neutralize a terrorist mastermind, earning a Congressional Medal of Honor in the process. I was just a kid from Norristown, Pennsylvania, who found a cat. But that doesn't mean there are no takeaways from my story. The overwhelming majority of us will never be war heroes, famous movie stars, legendary athletes, or influential politicians. In fact, if you look into your own lives, as I have done in writing this book, you will likely find that these types of people are not the ones who have shaped your life anyway. Most likely, your life has been shaped by everyday people: your family, your friends, your teachers, a coach. Each of us has a story to tell, and it is the combination of our stories that makes life interesting and meaningful.

I hope there were times while reading Silopi's story that you laughed and maybe even shed a tear. Ultimately, my story is one of life. We all have good days and bad days, and sometimes even terrifying days. We all experience the joys of realized dreams and the despair of crushing defeats. Our stories are all unique and important, and I thank you for listening to mine. I also hope you take the time to listen to the stories of those around you. In a world where we all too frequently communicate with one another by text, email, or social media, it can be easy to forget that we all come from someplace and have something important to say that cannot fit into the parameters of a Twitter (or X) post and which cannot be translated into a convenient abbreviation like "LOL" or "BRB." Take the time to listen to those stories; you just may learn something you hadn't already known. And for the younger generations, listen to what those ahead of you in life have gone through. It may open your eyes and spare you a life of preventable mistakes.

In writing this book, I have taken a deep look back into my life. If you have not done this yourself, it is an interesting endeavor. What I learned most in this exercise is that it is very easy to miss the forest for the trees. At the time you are dealing with a problem or trying to overcome a situation, the details of your life can become all-consuming. However, when you look back on things, especially with the hindsight of many years, you can see the path that was laid out for you all along. It is a plan that I believe is divinely set. Unfortunately, that does not always mean that the problems or circumstances are easy to overcome. This is where I think each of us can learn, or relearn, a critical virtue in our lives: resilience.

As society has progressed, many aspects of our lives have become easier. We are no longer forced to hunt for food or plant the crops we will later consume after harvest. Computers, cellphones, and the internet have made our lives astronomically easier, but they have also made the world much more complicated. The survival concerns of the past have been replaced by the technological concerns of the present. In short, while the generation just before your own may lament how easy you have it (an exercise you will also engage in one day), this does not mean that your life is free of trials and tribulations. After reflecting on my own story, I have come to realize that life is not easy for any of us.

Sadly, I believe that somewhere along the line, parents have unintentionally done their children a great disservice. They have left them with the misguided belief that life should be fun and devoid of any unpleasantness. In reality, life is not always fun. In fact, life is not even fun most of the time. For me, school was not fun. Basic Training and much of my time in the military were not fun. College was not fun. Crawling out of bed at four in the morning to battle traffic on the way to DC each day was not fun. Waiting in line, being sick, moving to a new residence, working overtime, punishing your children for their misdeeds, paying taxes—none of these things are fun. However, what gets most of us through these challenges is resilience. Coming to the realization that our obstacles in life are temporary is crucial. Resilience is the ability to stay in the fight until the obstacles pass. Looking back on my story, I realize that there were countless times when I could have quit. Giving up would have been the easiest thing to do. But that is not how winning is done. Winners keep going. That's resilience.

I can tell you that, although we have never met, you can do far more than you think you can. When someone tells you that you can't do something, don't listen. If I had listened to the FBI recruiter in Philadelphia who told me that I was too young to be an FBI agent and that I would never become an agent without a Master's degree, my life may have taken a drastically different turn. But, as I put the finishing touches on this book, I sit here as a retired FBI Special Agent, basking in the glow of a twenty-seven-year career. My career took me across the country and overseas. I helped with the case against the FBI's most notorious spy, Robert Hanssen. I huddled next to my car while pumping gas for fear that I could be the next target of the DC Sniper as John Allen Muhammad and Lee Boyd Malvo killed seventeen people and wounded ten others in the greater DC area, including the shopping center Kristen and I routinely frequented. I, along with the rest of the Washington Field Office personnel, were evacuated to the underground parking garage when Flight 93 was believed to be headed to the U.S. Capitol on September 11th. Hours later, I found myself standing next to the burning Pentagon as I prepared to conduct witness interviews. I went on to become a Crisis Negotiator and a Polygraph Examiner. I interviewed and interrogated bank robbers, murderers, kidnappers, child molesters, spies, and terrorists. Had I given up after listening to that recruiter so many years ago, none of this would have taken place. Don't listen to the naysayers. Fight for what you want. That's resilience.

During my time in the FBI, I also earned two Master's Degrees and a Ph.D. The kid who thought that service in the U.S. Army would be far less terrifying than going to college went on to earn four degrees beyond high school. Take my word for it: even if the naysayer is YOU, don't listen to them either. That's resilience.

As I put the finishing touches on this book, Kristen and I have just celebrated our twenty-fifth wedding anniversary. For many years, our relationship was built on a steady diet of unbridled excitement to see one another, quickly followed by the overwhelming sadness of leaving each other a few days later. As many of you probably already know, relationships—especially the most important ones—require resilience as well. Fight for those you love, and don't give up just because things get difficult. That's resilience.

We now seem to live in a world where no one can laugh at themselves, and laughing at someone else could conceivably violate state or federal law. As I wrote this book, I realized just how strong a role humor has played in my life, in the life of my family, and in my marriage. In my family, the good-natured ribbing could be directed at an eighty-year-old as easily as it could be at an eight-week-old. No one is safe, and no one gets out unscathed. There are two credos my family seem to live by: a) You only tease the ones you love; and b) There are no big heads in our family. I believe our country can benefit from a bit of each of these approaches to life. We could all stand to tease each other a little more, and it may benefit all of our growing egos if we can get back to laughing at ourselves a little more as well. This becomes a much easier task when we can once again connect on the simple reality that we are all Americans.

Looking back on my Army days, my units were much like my family. Everybody was a potential target of a joke, and everyone dished it out. I believe that fights did not erupt over this teasing and feelings remained relatively intact because we all realized that, regardless of our race, ethnicity, or state of origin, we were all soldiers first. Let's all learn to laugh again. That too is resilience.

Lastly, regardless of your religion or lack thereof, I can tell you that looking back on my life in the preceding pages, I see God's fingerprints throughout my journey. There are times when I have thanked God for the blessings in my life, and there are times when I shook an angry fist heavenward, wondering why my prayers went unanswered. However, it is not until I look back on the whole of my life that I see the many blessings I have missed due to my own momentary frustrations. Why was I stationed in Germany instead of Georgia? Why did I not get hired by that first police department? Why did Kristen and I have to live so far away from one another? Why did I not get that transfer back to Detroit? It is very easy to bemoan all of our disappointments when we are caught up in the moment. But for any and all of these efforts at second-guessing God's plan, I can also highlight a clear indication of His grace: being one of only 102 interns selected for the 1995 Honors Internship Program; Kristen being forced to wait a year to submit her intern application; both of us being assigned to the same unit; being assigned to the Detroit Division after first being offered New York City; being assigned to the Atlantic City office after my initial orders had me going to Newark Division Headquarters; and, of course, finding Silopi. For each unanswered prayer you may have complained about, there are likely countless others that you may have missed. Take the time to look for them. That is also a form of resilience.

A thorough diagram of my life's trajectory and the unmistakable divinity observed at the many waypoints along my path have left me confident that God has always had a plan for me. Thankfully, I realized this truth very early in my life. As a result, I have often prayed to Him:

"Dear Heavenly Father, I can only rejoice in whatever happens to me because I know you only want the best. I just pray that you give me enough strength to overcome whatever happens until I can see its glorious message."

Typing out this prayer for the first time and actually seeing it in print, I now realize that for a great portion of my life, I have been unwittingly asking God for resilience. I do not expect you to be a Christian or even to be religious, but this does not stop me from remaining confident in the knowledge that God also has a plan for your life and for the lives of those you love. I thank you from the very bottom of my heart for reading Silopi's story. I hope you enjoyed reading it as much as I enjoyed writing it. And, most importantly, I hope you walk away from it with the resilience to push through life's difficulties and the awareness to spot the little signs of love that exist all around you—especially those that can crawl into a dusty old Army hat.

ACKNOWLEDGEMENTS

There are many people I would like to thank for helping bring this story to life. For starters, I thank my beautiful wife, Kristen. As this story demonstrates, you changed my life in incalculable ways and I thank God for you daily. Thank you for your love and encouragement in writing this story. You are the best part of my life. Thank you as well to my handsome sons, Jack and Joey. You guys were a huge motivation in sharing this story. Reviewing my life as I wrote this book has helped me to realize that every twist, turn, and unexpected change of direction was leading me straight to you. You are the greatest blessing in the lives of your mother and me. We are incredibly proud of you both. Now, go out and write your own story.

My heartfelt thanks go out to my mother and father who, as can be clearly observed within the pages of this book, have always been there for me. Words cannot adequately express my appreciation for the life and love you have given me. I also offer thanks to my siblings and extended family who have always shared with me their love, their laughter, and their uncanny ability to tell a story. I also offer a special thanks to my dear, sweet mother-in-law, Irene, who not only sat and listened to every word of this story, but routinely begged for me to write more so that she could sit and listen. You are the world's greatest cheerleader!!!

A special thanks goes out to Dr. Annette Spencer for her continued willingness to review what I write and offer her helpful and important insights. You are as close to family as a person can be without a shared bloodline, and I am eternally grateful for your assistance and your place in our family. I would also like to thank Michael FitzGerald for his review of my manuscript, his recommendations, his years of wise counsel, and above all else, his friendship.

I also offer my profound thanks to the fine people at Defiance Press who not only love this great nation, but offer undying support to their writers. Dave Roberts had a vision when he formed this company and I am incredibly thankful to have found Defiance Press and to have been so warmly welcomed into the Defiance family. I especially would like to thank Mark Pruitt for bringing me into the fold and Lisa Woodward for smoothing out the rough edges in my writing. This is a better book because of you.

Lastly, I would like to thank two important groups of people. Thank you to the brave members of our military, past and present. Your selfless dedication to this country helps to ensure our freedoms. Thank you for what you do and for placing our safety as a nation above your own. May God forever bless you and your families and keep you all safe. Finally, thank you to the salt-of-the earth people of Norristown and Philadelphia, Pennsylvania. No matter where I may roam, you will forever be my home. Keep up the good fight, and don't take any crap from anyone. Go Phils and Go Birds!!!

www.ingramcontent.com/pod-product-compliance
Lightning Source LLC
Chambersburg PA
CBHW070342090426
42733CB00009B/1262